WhatsApp

Digital Media and Society Series

Nancy Baym, *Personal Connections in the Digital Age*, 2nd edition
Taina Bucher, *Facebook*
Mercedes Bunz and Graham Meikle, *The Internet of Things*
Jean Burgess and Joshua Green, *YouTube*, 2nd edition
Mark Deuze, *Media Work*
Andrew Dubber, *Radio in the Digital Age*
Quinn DuPont, *Cryptocurrencies and Blockchains*
Charles Ess, *Digital Media Ethics*, 3rd edition
Terry Flew, *Regulating Platforms*
Jordan Frith, *Smartphones as Locative Media*
Gerard Goggin, *Apps: From Mobile Phones to Digital Lives*
Alexander Halavais, *Search Engine Society*, 2nd edition
Martin Hand, *Ubiquitous Photography*
Robert Hassan, *The Information Society*
Kylie Jarrett, *Digital Labor*
Amelia Johns, Ariadna Matamoros-Fernández, and Emma Baulch, *WhatsApp: From a one-to-one Messaging App to a Global Communication Platform*
Tim Jordan, *Hacking*
D. Bondy Valdovinos Kaye, Jing Zeng and Patrik Wikström, *TikTok: Creativity and Culture in Short Video*
Graeme Kirkpatrick, *Computer Games and the Social Imaginary*
Tama Leaver, Tim Highfield and Crystal Abidin, *Instagram*
Leah A. Lievrouw, *Alternative and Activist New Media*, 2nd edition
Rich Ling and Jonathan Donner, *Mobile Communication*
Donald Matheson and Stuart Allan, *Digital War Reporting*
Nick Monaco and Samuel Woolley, *Bots*
Dhiraj Murthy, *Twitter*, 2nd edition
Zizi A. Papacharissi, *A Private Sphere: Democracy in a Digital Age*
Julian Thomas, Rowan Wilken and Ellie Rennie, *Wi-Fi*
Katrin Tiidenberg, Natalie Ann Hendry and Crystal Abidin, *tumblr*
Jill Walker Rettberg, *Blogging*, 2nd edition
Patrik Wikström, *The Music Industry*, 3rd edition

WhatsApp

From a one-to-one Messaging App
to a Global Communication Platform

AMELIA JOHNS
ARIADNA MATAMOROS-FERNÁNDEZ
EMMA BAULCH

polity

Copyright © Amelia Johns, Ariadna Matamoros-Fernández, and Emma Baulch 2024

The right of Amelia Johns, Ariadna Matamoros-Fernández, and Emma Baulch to be identified as Authors of this Work has been asserted in accordance with the UK Copyright, Designs and Patents Act 1988.

First published in 2024 by Polity Press

Polity Press
65 Bridge Street
Cambridge CB2 1UR, UK

Polity Press
111 River Street
Hoboken, NJ 07030, USA

All rights reserved. Except for the quotation of short passages for the purpose of criticism and review, no part of this publication may be reproduced, stored in a retrieval system or transmitted, in any form or by any means, electronic, mechanical, photocopying, recording or otherwise, without the prior permission of the publisher.

ISBN-13: 978-1-5095-5052-4
ISBN-13: 978-1-5095-5053-1(pb)

A catalogue record for this book is available from the British Library.

Typeset in 10.25 on 13pt Scala
by Fakenham Prepress Solutions, Fakenham, Norfolk NR21 8NL
Printed and bound in Great Britain by TJ Books Ltd, Padstow, Cornwall

The publisher has used its best endeavours to ensure that the URLs for external websites referred to in this book are correct and active at the time of going to press. However, the publisher has no responsibility for the websites and can make no guarantee that a site will remain live or that the content is or will remain appropriate.

Every effort has been made to trace all copyright holders, but if any have been overlooked the publisher will be pleased to include any necessary credits in any subsequent reprint or edition.

For further information on Polity, visit our website:
politybooks.com

Contents

Figures and Tables vi
Acknowledgements viii

Introduction 1
1 Why WhatsApp Matters 18
2 Platform Biography 46
3 Everyday Uses of WhatsApp 75
4 WhatsApp Publics 104
5 WhatsApp Business Model 134
6 WhatsApp Futures 156

Notes 175
References 181
Index 202

Figures and Tables

FIGURES

0.1 WhatsApp official account tweet during the 2021 outage   2
0.2 Artist's impression of WhatsApp's chat groups   7
2.1 Artist's impression of the landing page of WhatsApp's business solution   68
3.1 Artist's impression of "Good morning" messages and inspirational quotes which circulate in family WhatsApp groups   83
3.2 Artist's impression of a group chat interface showing a notification that a user has left the group   97
3.3 Artist's impression of a sticker showing Jesus Christ with the accompanying sentence: "Jesus knows what your deleted message said", and a sticker used to joke about messages that your group members ignore, which shows the double tick blue read receipt with the accompanying sentence: "your message was successfully ignored"   98
4.1 Photograph taken by Amelia (July, 2018) of an informant's family group chat, and a chain mail message containing misinformation, which circulated prior to Malaysian 14th General Election.   106
4.2 Australian Government official Coronavirus WhatsApp channel   117
4.3 Artist's impression of advertisements on the open

web selling registered phone numbers to enable mass messaging on WhatsApp 124
5.1 Artist's impression of 'Business Tools' available on WhatsApp for Business. In the 'Business Tools' section within the Business App, the option to advertise on Facebook and Instagram is prominent 144
6.1 Artist's impression of WhatsApp's landing page in January 2014 based on website stored by the Web Archive (https://web.archive.org/web/20140102070018/https://www.whatsapp.com/) 164

Tables

1.1 WhatsApp users by country 2023 20
5.1 Growth of WhatsApp business users and customers, in numbers 136

Acknowledgements

This book has its beginnings in a workshop held at the School of Arts and Social Sciences, Monash University Malaysia in November 2018. Emma and Ariadna had discussed the idea of holding a workshop on WhatsApp when they worked together at Queensland University of Technology (QUT), and when Emma moved to Malaysia in mid-2018 she applied for funds to invite Amelia, who had been studying WhatsApp's role in anti-government political organizing in Malaysia, as part of a post-doctoral appointment at Deakin University. Others who presented at the workshop included Natalie Pang and Pauline Leong, and we would like to thank these two scholars for their contributions. We also thank the School of Arts and Social Sciences for providing funds to support the workshop. The workshop resulted in a five-year collaboration between Emma, Amelia and Ariadna on various publications and projects studying WhatsApp, including this book.

Amelia would like to also extend very warm thanks to Deakin University for funding the three-year postdoctoral appointment that led to her collaboration with Emma and Ariadna. Deakin University offered seed grant funding towards her project examining digital citizenship and activism among Malaysian youth from 2016 to 2018. She would particularly like to thank Niki Cheong, who was her research assistant on the project, and with whom she has collaborated on several other projects and publications focused on WhatsApp in Malaysia. She would also like to thank colleagues and friends at University of Technology Sydney, where she is now located. Similarly, Ariadna would also like to express her gratitude to her colleagues, mentors and friends at QUT, and especially to the Digital Media Research Centre (DMRC) and Jean Burgess, for creating a nourishing and welcoming research community.

Soon after the workshop, we began work on a special issue on WhatsApp, which appeared in 2020 in the open access journal *First Monday*, titled 'Ten years of WhatsApp: The role of chat apps in the formation and mobilisation of online publics' (Baulch et al., 2020). We would like to thank contributors to that special issue for their interest in working with us. They include: Edgar Gómez Cruz and Ramaswami Harindranath, Stefania Milan and Sérgio Barbosa, Natalie Pang and Yue Ting Woo, Marcelo Santos, Magdalena Saldaña and Andrés Rosenberg, and Emiliano Treré. When WhatsApp changed its privacy settings in 2019, we published a commentary in *The Conversation*, titled 'Becoming more like WhatsApp won't solve Facebook's woes – here's why'. In the same year Natalie Pang invited us to contribute a chapter on messaging apps to the *Research Handbook on Social Media and Society* (Edward Elgar), co-edited by Natalie and Marko Skoric. The volume appeared in 2023, with our chapter titled 'A survey of media and communications scholarship on messaging apps'. We thank Natalie and Marko for this opportunity. Also in 2019, with Fiona Suwana, Ariadna and Emma undertook a study of the use of WhatsApp in Indonesia's general election campaign, which was published in *New Media and Society* in 2022. The paper was presented as part of a panel Amelia, Emma and Ariadna organized at the Association of Internet Researchers conference in Brisbane in 2019. Subsequently, a member of the audience, Crystal Abidin, approached us to pitch a proposal for a book on WhatsApp to Polity's Digital Media and Society series. Crystal, one of the authors of a book on Instagram published in the same series in 2020, had been asked by series editor Mary Savigar to suggest names of scholars who could write such a book. We had our first meeting with Mary in October 2019, and, scattered across three different locations, began to slowly draft the book to completion over a two-year period. We thank Mary for patiently and persistently guiding us through this process, and the anonymous reviewers for contributing valuable feedback to several drafts. We thank Crystal for recommending us to Mary.

We would like to also extend thanks to Gabriel Pereira for undertaking interviews with WhatsApp users in Malaysia for the book, and to Paul Byron, who read and provided feedback on the manuscript. We would also like to thank the illustrator of the book, Phoebe Tan, who turned around our late request for illustrations in an incredibly timely and professional manner.

Finally, we would like to give our gratitude to our friends and family. Without their support we would not be able to put in the long hours that go towards a book collaboration such as this, coordinated across time zones and busy lives. Amelia would especially like to thank her partner, Paulina, for her patience and love. Emma thanks her colleagues, friends and her daughter in Malaysia for making it such a comfortable place from which to produce scholarship. Finally, Ariadna would like to thank her partner, Àlex, for his love and encouragement. WhatsApp is part of our stories in many unique and fun ways. We are delighted to share these stories and those of users we interviewed.

Introduction

On Tuesday 5 October 2021, at 11.40am Eastern time, people around the world discovered that they could not access Facebook, Instagram and WhatsApp – with all three of the Meta-owned platforms seeming to have been wiped from the internet. For many, who use these platforms as their main connection to friends, family, news and businesses around the world, this amounted to a social blackout. Users flocked to Twitter* to find out what had happened, as reported in the media and by Twitter's official accounts who cheekily tweeted 'Hello literally everyone'.[1] Meta (formerly Facebook) executives were forced to explain the cause of the outage via their official accounts on Twitter, and reassure users that they were working on the problem. Rivals took the opportunity to respond with humour. In response to the tweet from WhatsApp's official Twitter account, one user @mentioned Telegram and asked suggestively if the Russian-owned app was 'single', to which Telegram replied: 'come over, the servers are up and my parents aren't home' (figure 0.1).

But for all the playfulness, the outage posed serious questions. First, the difference in tone of tweets from WhatsApp users from around the world highlighted the uneven impact the outage had on the social lives of users, with an evident discrepancy between users in the Global South who shared stories of businesses and families disrupted, and

---

* Twitter was rebranded as X in July 2023. However, we decided to refer to X as Twitter throughout the book since this is the name the platform had at the time of writing.

Introduction

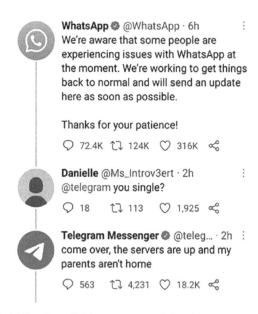

Figure 0.1: WhatsApp official account tweet during the 2021 outage. Screenshot taken by Amelia, 6 October, 2021.

those in the Global North. In many countries, WhatsApp has risen to become more than a one-to-one communication app, or a privacy-focused alternative to other social media platforms. With its low data usage and generous data plans, private and public group chats, media sharing and digital payment and business functions, it has been referred to as an essential communication 'utility' (Gajjala & Verma, 2018), whose ubiquity and embeddedness in the daily life of users becomes especially apparent when it breaks down.

Media reports further contextualized the uneven impact of the outage, with stories from Latin America and Africa speaking of more acute impacts than in North America and Europe, or Asian countries, where, due to time zone differences, the outage hit during the night (Zhong & Satariano, 2021). For the former, users experienced up to seven hours of lost business revenue (Waldron, 2021), doctors were unable to book appointments with patients (Talmazan, 2021) and large parts of an informal worker economy that operates through WhatsApp came to a grinding halt, resulting in groceries not being delivered, and taxis and ride shares being unable to operate (Froio, 2021). In Africa, where WhatsApp is so essential to daily life (Hassan & Hitchen, 2022) that, in some countries, you can use it to renew your car licence (Rall, 2022), conspiracy theories started to circulate that governments were blocking the platform. In Tanzania the scale of public panic was such that a government spokesperson took to Twitter to urge the public to 'stay calm' (Schwikowski, 2021). The outage showed how WhatsApp has become so integral to many people's daily rhythms and interactions, that losing access to it feels like being locked out of social life.

In this book we argue that WhatsApp is more than a simple messaging app – it is a global communication and business platform that converges personal, public and commercial contexts. As a reader, when you think about WhatsApp, you might have in mind the simple WhatsApp mobile application for chatting with friends and family, which is easily downloaded from the app store. But in this book, we refer to WhatsApp as a platform. Our use of the term 'platform' conceptualizes WhatsApp as a complex technical system that brings together a number of different stakeholders: businesses, ordinary users, news organizations and public officials, for example. Nieborg and Helmond (2019) use the term 'instances' to refer to the different technical and economic components that allow companies like Meta to perform the 'extraction, analysis and distribution of data [that] is central to [Meta's] business model' (p. 199). By focusing on the Messenger app as one of Meta's 'instances', the authors demonstrate not only how Messenger evolved into a service that has platform properties of its own but also how it is a key component of Meta's 'platformization' (Nieborg & Helmond, 2019, p. 202). On the one hand, Meta extends its boundaries into the web and mobile ecosystem via the development of social plug-ins and multiple apps. On the other hand, it opens up its programmable infrastructure to third-party developers and organizations so that they can create a presence for themselves within Meta's family of platform 'instances' (e.g., Facebook, Instagram, WhatsApp and Messenger) (p. 202). In this process, Meta is able to turn user data (primarily of ordinary users) into a commodity form that is made available to other end-users (businesses, advertisers), which fuels the company's growth (p. 197).

Nieborg and Helmond argue that studying Facebook Messenger can help us understand important elements of Meta's industrial development. In this book, we do not limit our analysis to the role WhatsApp is playing in the 'bigger' story of Meta's evolution. Rather, we centre our discussion on WhatsApp's evolution as a platform in its own right, arguing that WhatsApp has acquired too much technical, economic and social weight to be accurately described as an 'instance' of Meta. WhatsApp's evolution as a platform is not only shaped by its technological expansion (which we unpack in chapter 2), or by its economic and business dimensions (which we explore in chapters 1 and 5), but also by how users have adapted it in various ways in different parts of the word, which we describe in chapters 3 and 4. The social uses of WhatsApp and the elements of user agency that are inherent in them are of crucial importance to our understanding of WhatsApp's place in media landscapes in the present, as well as its significance within histories of platform ecosystems and their evolution. For this reason, the book makes space for understanding not only how WhatsApp advances Meta's business interests, but also its meanings for ordinary users, and how they may extend its possibilities. The book addresses the following research questions: How has WhatsApp evolved from a one-to-one chat app to a global communication and business platform? And why is it important to study WhatsApp as a platform?

To answer our research questions, we use tweets, media reports, corporate information and historical artefacts such as saved websites from the Internet Archive, as well as published scholarship. We also draw on interviews we have conducted with WhatsApp users in three countries where the platform has had a significant uptake: Malaysia, Indonesia and Spain.[2] These sites were chosen because we have grown up in or lived in these places where WhatsApp use is ubiquitous, or have undertaken extensive research on WhatsApp communication practices in these sites. Ariadna is from Barcelona (Spain) and has been using WhatsApp since its early beginnings. For her, WhatsApp is the main communication platform she uses to stay in touch with family and friends. Amelia began using WhatsApp in 2016 while conducting fieldwork in Malaysia. She has since been embedded in activist groups on WhatsApp and has used it in her personal life, where it is the main way she communicates with her partner's extended family in Mexico. Emma found her use of WhatsApp intensified after she moved to Malaysia in 2018. Then, it assumed the role of a family communication platform where she, her mother and siblings regularly update one another on their lives and share photos. It also became central to her social life in Malaysia: Emma participates in WhatsApp book club groups, hiking groups, tennis groups, meditation groups and neighbourhood groups. She uses it to chat with her Kuala Lumpur friends, organize dinners, outings and dates, as well as to book appointments with her accountant, her dentist, her masseuse and her psychotherapist.

WhatsApp as a platform

Our analytical framework for conceptualizing WhatsApp as a platform is organized into three parts. In its *economic dimension*, WhatsApp has evolved from a popular though largely unprofitable chat application to become a multi-sided market under Meta's ownership, that facilitates interactions between ordinary users, businesses (e.g., small businesses, content producers), advertisers and institutions (governments, banks, political parties, media). Microeconomics theory and platform studies scholarship (Bucher, 2012; Gawer, 2014; Nieborg & Helmond, 2019; Rieder & Sire, 2014; Rochet & Tirole, 2003) consider how, by leveraging and monetizing exchanges between diverse end-users, technologies (and their business owners) are able to grow their user base exponentially, 'capture' new markets and consolidate media power (Nieborg & Helmond, 2019, p. 200).

One framing that may help us to understand how WhatsApp business solutions contribute to Meta's economic growth is provided by Athique (2019). He argues that a contemporary phase of development in platform economies revolves around digital transactions for which platforms receive a commission. This refers to the way platforms extract value through the integration of mobile payments like QPay and e-wallets, adding a 'layer' of functionality that Athique (2019, p. 6) refers to as 'transactional'. This evolution of WhatsApp into a *business platform* is consistent with Meta's broader ambition to extend its media dominance beyond the web, into the mobile ecosystem (Goggin, 2014; Nieborg & Helmond, 2019). This will be the focus of chapters 1 and 5.

In its *technical dimension*, WhatsApp has undergone rapid transformation to facilitate interactions between these diverse end-users. By explaining WhatsApp's technological expansion into the open web and the mobile ecosystem, we wish to challenge the conventional understanding of WhatsApp as simply a mobile chat app. Consistent with other platform studies scholars (Bodle, 2011; Burgess & Baym, 2020; Gerlitz & Helmond, 2013; Gillespie, 2018; Nieborg & Helmond, 2019), we focus on specific technological features to explain the evolution of technologies into platforms. For example, in the case of WhatsApp, its core mobile chat app is central to WhatsApp's business model – after all, more than 2 billion users are active on the chatting app (see table 1.1, chapter 1). But WhatsApp also has other 'app instances' (Nieborg & Helmond, 2019, p. 199): the WhatsApp Desktop app, which people can download to their computers to chat without having to use their mobile phones, and a mobile app that targets small businesses – the WhatsApp Business App. Within WhatsApp's 'app ecosystem' (Nieborg & Helmond, 2019, p. 197), the platform also offers a set of application programming interfaces[3] (APIs) – such as the Business API, as well as plug-ins (e.g., WhatsApp Share Button, the Click to Chat Button), and software development kits[4] (SDKs). Further, WhatsApp has various 'web instances' (Nieborg & Helmond, 2019, p. 199): its main website (whatsapp.com), a computer-based extension of the core mobile app – the WhatsApp Web (web.whatsapp.com), and a site to showcase its business products (business.whatsapp.com). Acknowledging this technological evolution (the focus of chapter 2) allows us to offer a holistic picture of WhatsApp as a platform.

Importantly, our conceptualization of WhatsApp as a platform also involves a *social dimension*. In the book we pay attention to the evolution of communication practices attached

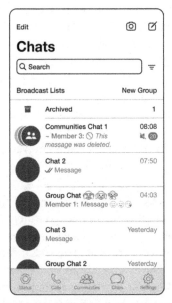

Figure 0.2: Artist's impression of WhatsApp's chat groups. Art provided by Phoebe Tan.

to WhatsApp, while also considering how WhatsApp enables and extends the ways people engage in social life. Scholars like Burgess and Baym (2020) and Gillespie (2018) suggest that media technologies grow or fail owing to the social participation and agency of users. Users commit their time and resources to produce the 'communicative or expressive content' that define platform cultures, and to debate, contest, resist or reinforce existing social norms (p. 17). As Gillespie claims, users 'don't simply walk the paths laid out by the ... platforms. They push against them, swarm over them, and imbue them with new meanings' (Gillespie, 2018, p. 23). By encouraging user appropriation WhatsApp has also invited illegal and harmful uses, prompting calls for action towards better regulation of platforms to limit the spread of harmful content. By focusing on these social dimensions, our book regards WhatsApp not just as a business or a technical architecture, but as an 'intermediar[y] between content and users ... and ultimately as media' (Rieder & Sire, 2014, p. 202; see also Bucher, 2012; Gillespie, 2018).

Gómez Cruz and Harindranath (2020) use the concept 'technology of life' to 'highlight the ways in which life is expanded, experienced, and has become increasingly dependent' on WhatsApp in many countries of the Global South. For them, any analysis of WhatsApp should provide a contextual and historical analysis of how the platform is experienced by different groups in various geographic regions, which we offer in chapters 3 and 4. WhatsApp's core mobile app's unique design (e.g., groups, encryption) and affordances (e.g., simple interface, low data usage, free service), among other controversial commercial partnerships outlined in chapter 1, have facilitated its widespread uptake by diverse cohorts in countries such as India, Brazil, Indonesia, Malaysia, Kenya, South Africa, Italy and Spain. Some features introduced by WhatsApp, such as Group invite links, which allow users to publish links on the open web to encourage public discussions, have become hugely popular in countries like Brazil (Caetano et al., 2018), while remaining relatively unknown to users in other parts of the world. The uneven character of uptake points to the important role social context plays in shaping uses of WhatsApp and its design, and highlights the dynamic relationship users have with the platform as they seek to mould it to their social, political and business needs, as we show in chapters 2 and 4. In order to understand WhatsApp's global spread and development as a platform, we consider how users in different cultural contexts have played an active part in making it relevant to those contexts and contributed to its technological evolution.

In the regions of its largest uptake, WhatsApp as a platform is 'sticky' – a term used by Chen et al. to describe the Chinese platform, WeChat (Chen et al., 2018). Stickiness arises not from loyalty to the platform, but because people's social contacts, cherished memories and experiences, news, political talk and commercial transactions all happen in one place, making it a 'social, informational, transactional and ... infrastructural' hub (p. 16). Like WeChat, WhatsApp has become a platform with add-ons and services that make it increasingly difficult for users to leave. The concept of 'network effects' can help us to understand this stickiness. Network effects describe the way a service grows its value exponentially as new end-users join. For example, the growing popularity of WhatsApp as a 'go to' platform for connecting with a diverse range of contacts raises 'switching costs', which pertain to the inconvenience felt by users if they abandon WhatsApp for another platform (Nieborg & Helmond, 2019, p. 211; Bucher, 2021). High switching costs render the platform valuable because they increase user dependence on it, making it an attractive prospect for business users wanting to grow their client base. However, in this book we argue that network effects and switching costs are not the only factors that make WhatsApp sticky. The concept of 'platform vernaculars' (Gibbs et al., 2015) is also important to understanding how users become 'glued' to WhatsApp, not only because switching costs are high, but also because the platform accommodates users' social and emotional needs, ranging from self-expression, care, humour and intimacy to platform-specific ways of participating in civic life and political organizing. These uses are highlighted in detail in chapters 3 and 4, and we argue that these dimensions need to be taken into consideration in accounting for WhatsApp's success.

In its very stickiness, WhatsApp resembles chat-based superapps such as LINE, KakaoTalk and WeChat, all of which developed transactional dimensions, including in-app sale of products and services and in-app pay functions, well before WhatsApp did. But there are also key differences that distinguish WhatsApp from these 'superapps'. Superapps have been defined predominantly as single, user-facing apps that operate mainly on mobile devices and converge interpersonal communication with commercial services (Chen et al., 2018; Steinberg, 2020). In some ways, WhatsApp conforms to this definition, as it is increasingly bundling services within the main chat app and shares many features with technologies like WeChat that, socially, are *'experienced* as a vernacular, everyday infrastructure' (Steinberg et al., 2022, p. 1411). Technically, though, WhatsApp is only a 'do-everything app' (Steinberg et al., 2022, p. 1407) for ordinary users, who experience all WhatsApp's services in one interface. Companies need to download the WhatsApp Business App or use extensions such as the WhatsApp Business API to facilitate e-commerce via chat with customers. Despite this and other differences, tracing WhatsApp's evolution alongside the development of Asian superapps, as we do in chapter 1, is useful to our argument that WhatsApp has evolved from a one-on-one chat app into a global communication and business platform. Geography matters to WhatsApp's metamorphosis into a platform, in terms of user uptake in the Global South, competition with Asian superapps and regulatory contexts around the world, all shaping its and Meta's trajectory.

In this book we follow these lines of development for WhatsApp, charting its rise and domination of rival messaging apps in terms of active users (WhatsApp, 2 billion, WeChat, 1.3 billion, Facebook Messenger, 988 million, QQ, 574 million, Telegram, 550 million) and how it has also surpassed most social media platforms, with WhatsApp having the third largest number of active users of a 'social platform' in the world in January 2022 (We Are Social, 2022).

The importance of studying WhatsApp as a platform

WhatsApp has been conceptualized in mobile media studies as a single, user-facing, instant messaging app that exists as part of an app ecology or mobile ecosystem – with the rise of the smartphone and the app store defining its trajectory as a technology (Goggin, 2006, 2021; Ling & Lai, 2016; Ling et al., 2020; Morris & Murray, 2018). In this book we argue that WhatsApp has outgrown this narrow definition to become a global communication and business platform hosting numerous app and web instances of its own (to use Nieborg and Helmond's term), and connecting a wide array of end-users in the private and public exchange of information, content and financial transactions.

By tracing this evolution, the book makes three contributions. First, by representing the economic, technical and social complexity of WhatsApp, we expand current scholarly representations of WhatsApp as just a simple and private chatting app. Platform studies associates the increasing dominance of Silicon Valley platforms in the late 2000s and early 2010s (Google, YouTube, Facebook and Twitter) with a paradigmatic shift in the power relations between tech giants, the market, government and civil society. Within the broader field of 'platform studies', there is growing interest in studying how platforms change over time, and in challenging any notion of them as static entities. To date, analyses of WhatsApp have largely been absent from the body of work seeking to conceptualize platforms, and there has been a general reluctance to view mobile 'apps' as platforms in their own right. Nieborg and Helmond (2019) examined Facebook's Messenger app as both a platform and an 'instance' of Meta, but no such study of WhatsApp exists. That is, work that seeks to periodize the evolution of platforms is yet to consider how WhatsApp's rise might be implicated in such periodization. For example, Bucher's (2021) book about Facebook considers this platform a 'global operating system and serious political, economic and cultural power broker' (p. 3), but WhatsApp to date has not been part of this discussion. In this book, we show how WhatsApp is accruing significant 'political, economic and cultural power' in many parts of the world, making it increasingly pivotal to Meta's own commercial ambitions, and paving the way for future scholarship which seeks to understand WhatsApp's role in contemporary platform ecosystems.

Our second contribution, and part of our supporting evidence for the argument that WhatsApp constitutes a platform, involves the way in which it has long operated as *social media* in many parts of the world. Burgess et al. (2017) define social media technologies as 'digital platforms, services and apps built around the convergence of content sharing, public communication, and interpersonal connection' (p. 1), and WhatsApp fits this definition well. In countries like Brazil and India, for example, a typical WhatsApp user will use the core chatting app to socialize with family, friends and acquaintances, but also to access news, get updates from public servants, communicate with strangers on WhatsApp public groups, and communicate with small businesses (Saboia, 2016; Soeyuenmez, 2022). Meta's purchase of WhatsApp in 2014 incorporated new 'social' features, such as status (similar to Instagram Stories, which allow users to share 'public' ephemeral stories to all their contacts), video and group calling, and stickers to enhance these more social uses of the core mobile communication app. 'Broadcasting' and 'public' communication features were also gradually added at this time, transforming WhatsApp into a tool for political communication and, concerningly, information disorder. This has brought WhatsApp and Meta into the crosshairs of International regulators, with these features and their appropriation highlighting its resemblance to other social media platforms.

Third, WhatsApp's platformization reveals a new phase in Meta's industrial development – one in which WhatsApp's infrastructure, user cultures and its business model are intersecting and creating lines of tension that are important for internet researchers and media and communication scholars to grapple with. Mark Zuckerberg is committed to transforming WhatsApp into a service for businesses via the WhatsApp Business App and API, and a source of monetization for Meta, to the point that WhatsApp is presented as the 'next chapter' in the company's history (Munk, 2022). In 2019, Zuckerberg stated that WhatsApp was a key piece of Meta's 'privacy-focused vision for social networking' (Zuckerberg, 2019a). This is a shift that imagines the future of social media platforms to be one where privacy-focused communication platforms are integrated with today's open platforms, and is reflected in Mark Zuckerberg's plans to merge WhatsApp and the company's other platforms – Facebook, Instagram, Messenger – into a more integrated service. WhatsApp's motto of 'connecting the world privately'[5] aligns with Meta's vision to capitalize on social media's shift towards more private, ephemeral communication platforms. Meta's move to introduce end-to-end encryption on WhatsApp in 2016 sought to position WhatsApp as a trusted platform for activists and pro-democracy campaigners by using the same encryption protocol as Signal, WhatsApp's rival, and a trusted app for activists in North American and European markets (Santos & Faure, 2018). This pleased user demand for privacy-oriented applications. Yet, as we argue, WhatsApp (and Meta) strategically use encryption to obscure other aspects of its design and technological development that undermine user privacy (see also Santos & Faure, 2018). In this book, we seek to understand WhatsApp's evolution by positioning the platform in the context of Meta's ambitions to monetize WhatsApp by turning it into a business platform, which has consequences for user privacy.

Structure of the book

We begin by contextualizing WhatsApp's origins in relation to the development of the smartphone and the emergence of messaging apps as key media objects within the mobile ecosystem. Chapter 1 traces WhatsApp's emergence and departure from a range of early East Asian (LINE, Kakao Talk, WeChat) and North American (Telegram, Snapchat, Signal) messaging apps and pays particular attention to the significant changes leading up to and following its purchase by Meta in 2014. Understanding this metamorphosis can tell us much about the current status of WhatsApp in relation to other rivals in the messaging app ecosystem, and also sheds light on the trajectory of Meta's industrial development. The chapter focuses on the impact of Free Basics[6] as a commercial strategy aimed at monopolizing emerging markets, which consolidated WhatsApp's position as the default communication platform for many users in the Global South. We also consider the transformation of messaging apps, such as WhatsApp and its closest rival, WeChat, via efforts to monetize interaction among diverse end users. This illustrates similar but distinct strategies by dominant market players to kill off competitors and consolidate economic power. This competition, we argue, is transforming platform economies and is key to Meta's ambitions for WhatsApp.

This sets the scene for chapter 2, which adopts the approach of digital media scholars (e.g., Bucher, 2021; Burgess & Baym, 2020; Nieborg & Helmond, 2019) of using key technological features of platforms as proxies to understand their evolution. The chapter identifies three types of features that are key to participating in WhatsApp: intimacy and privacy-oriented features (including the Group feature, Communities and encryption); broadcast and shareability features (including sharing plug-ins, the Forward feature and the Broadcast list); and business-oriented features (including the Business App and API). We explain when WhatsApp introduced these features, why they are important for conceptualizing WhatsApp as a platform, and how users have contributed to their evolution. Our argument is that WhatsApp's technical evolution as a platform owes much to how it is used in key markets such as India, Brazil, Spain, Malaysia and Indonesia, to name a few.

In chapter 3, we consider the social dimension of WhatsApp, through a focus on everyday practices that have evolved on the platform as its network has grown in size and complexity. We adopt the term 'platform vernacular' from Gibbs et al. (2015) to describe how users appropriate features of the platform to construct it as a cultural space, replete with humour, intimacy, care and also less desirable elements of culture such as racist stereotypes. We argue that examining platform vernaculars offers a perspective on WhatsApp's success that goes beyond the concept of network effects, by which the value of platforms correlates to the size of their networks. A focus on platform vernacular highlights the emotion and creativity that keep users 'glued' to WhatsApp, making it 'sticky' (Chen et al., 2018). We discuss three categories of everyday practice that characterize WhatsApp as a site of platform vernacular: connection/disconnection, expression and public display.

Chapter 4 considers WhatsApp's role in public communication, including its use for activism and for news, journalism and political campaigning. The chapter examines how WhatsApp affords users security, coordination and broadcasting capabilities, and being 'up to date' with the news.

We draw attention to both the positive and negative implications of the role WhatsApp is playing in public discourse. On the one hand, it presents low entry barriers for engaging online. Therefore, it facilitates widespread participation in public discourse and civic life, and works to enhance and support key institutions of democracy. On the other hand, the platform is vulnerable to manipulation by social actors who seek to leverage its technological features, widespread use and everyday qualities to surreptitiously manipulate public discourse in the interest of powerful individuals and institutions. This has made WhatsApp a site for increasing 'information disorder' (Wardle & Derakhshan, 2017), leading to calls for greater content moderation as WhatsApp has fallen foul of regulators around the world.

In chapter 5 we explore the economic dimension of WhatsApp. We examine the evolution of WhatsApp as a platform for small and large businesses, offering services that facilitate customer relations management, through large-scale broadcast messaging, product display, one-on-one chats with individual customers and, in some places, monetary transactions. We discuss how these features expand out into the web, and draw the web into WhatsApp, through greater integration of WhatsApp Business clients and services with the advertising services of Facebook and Instagram. The chapter highlights key elements of WhatsApp's platformization, discusses how these processes enable WhatsApp to monetize its widespread use, and argues that such monetization is key to Meta's growth. The chapter draws on accounts from users in India and Brazil, where users can send money and pay for things using WhatsApp, to better understand how these new functions and elements tailored for business use affect ordinary user experiences. This sheds light on whether users are receptive to the new functionality of WhatsApp or whether they are concerned about the key trade-off, i.e., privacy.

In chapter 6, we conclude the book by reflecting on the story we present about how WhatsApp has changed and evolved from its inception to the present day as a global communication and business platform. We draw on this reflection to consider the future for WhatsApp. We address key questions about this future, delving into the meaning of Mark Zuckerberg's characterizations of WhatsApp as Meta's 'next chapter', and considering key challenges to WhatsApp's platformization and economic success, including the efforts of regulators to limit its growth, and its ability to compete with other platforms in key markets. Finally, we ask whether, for ordinary users, WhatsApp has moved too far away from the original vision laid out by Koum and Acton – WhatsApp's founders – of a simple, reliable communication app, with its business and public communication dimensions threatening to transform user experience into one altogether spammier, messier, less safe and less reliable.

I
Why WhatsApp Matters

Since its launch in 2009, and following Meta's purchase for the astronomical figure of $19 billion in 2014 (Olson, 2014), WhatsApp has become essential to individuals' and organizations' communication needs around the world. For the vast majority of its users, WhatsApp supports mundane and ephemeral forms of sociality and connectedness, with the circulation of jokes, news, stickers, 'praying chains', memes and 'Good morning' messages being popular cultural forms that foster intimacy, connection and joy between close and sometimes distant loved ones (Gajjala & Verma, 2018; Gómez Cruz & Harindranath, 2020; Karapanos et al., 2016). This was evident during the COVID-19 pandemic, where the volume of daily WhatsApp messages grew to 2.5 times that of normal usage, indicating the role this technology played in keeping people connected during the crisis (Seufert et al., 2022). WhatsApp became a platform to maintain connections with family and friends, but also to facilitate classroom education and work, as stay-at-home public health orders came into effect (Feldmann et al., 2021). It provided a lifeline to businesses forced to close during extended lockdowns, with reports from Latin America indicating a growth in business communication with customers. WhatsApp's business and pay integrations transformed WhatsApp into a vital sales channel for companies in Mexico and Brazil.[1] Indicating its more nefarious uses, high volumes of health misinformation also began circulating through the platform, leading Singaporean (Basu, 2020), Australian (Brown, 2020) and Indian governments (Singh, 2020a) to set up dedicated

WhatsApp channels and chatbots to try to counter the rising tide.

As these examples show, WhatsApp matters because it is part of the fabric of daily social life in many parts of the world, especially in the Global South. Since its early years, it has been hailed as a safe space for activists to organize and discuss politics (Pang & Woo, 2020), and a global distribution platform for news and entertainment (Boczek & Kloppers, 2020, p. 126; Newman et al., 2018). It also matters because in some regions it is evolving to become a critical platform for business and an essential tool for governments and organizations to communicate with the public (Basu, 2020; Singh, 2020a). But equally, uses of the platform that perpetuate harm also matter, since problematic practices arising from design changes, such as encryption, or changes to privacy and data-sharing policies, have led to highly publicized clashes between Meta and contesting social forces, including civil society, governments, regulators, media industries, human rights organizations and others. The multifaceted uses of WhatsApp and the debates they ignite are an important focus of this book and help answer the question of why WhatsApp matters.

Although it was founded in the US by Acton and Koum, WhatsApp's popularity grew fastest in non-English-speaking countries in Latin America (Gómez Cruz & Harindranath, 2020; Matassi et al., 2019; Pereira & Bojzuk, 2018; Saboia, 2016), India (Gajjala & Verma, 2018; Venkataramakrishnan, 2015), Southeast Asia (Ling & Lai, 2016; Tapsell, 2018) and Europe (Gil de Zúñiga et al., 2021; Vincent, 2014). In many of these regions, WhatsApp became popular because of its low data usage and low cost relative to standard phone calls and SMS (Gómez Cruz & Harindranath, 2020; Tapsell, 2018). In addition, smartphone usage in these markets had just begun to take off when WhatsApp was introduced, with low-cost smartphones entering into countries that had not experienced the home PC revolution, turning them into 'mobile-first' markets. Without a natural competitor, WhatsApp grew enormously in these countries and regions. By contrast, users in the US and Global North markets did not have the same motivation to switch to WhatsApp. For them, most data plans came with unlimited SMS, meaning an alternative messaging service was not needed. Secondly, users in the US had already experienced the PC revolution and established many of their social networks on web-based social media such as Facebook, Twitter and Skype (McMillan, 2014). This meant that the 'switching costs' (see Introduction) exceeded the benefit of setting up their networks anew on WhatsApp.

WhatsApp's simple design further contributed to its wide appeal (see table 1.1), with users only requiring a mobile phone number to register an account, while the interface mimicked SMS with some additional features, making it familiar (Baulch et al., 2020; Gajjala & Verma, 2018). As more social features were added, WhatsApp became so integrated into daily routines in many contexts that people relied on it in order to function in everyday life (Gómez Cruz & Harindranath, 2020).

Table 1.1: WhatsApp users by country 2023

Rank	Name of country	Number of WhatsApp users in 2023
#1	India	487 million
#2	Brazil	118 million
#3	Indonesia	85 million
#4	United States	79 million
#5	Russia	67 million
#6	Mexico	60 million
#7	Germany	49 million
#8	Italy	37 million
#9	Spain	32 million
#10	Argentina	26 million

Source: World Population Review (2023) at: https://worldpopulationreview.com/country-rankings/whatsapp-users-by-country. Table created by the authors.

Since Meta's purchase of WhatsApp, its reach and its meaning to users in key markets has evolved, becoming about much more than interpersonal communication. Instead, it has grown into a platform supporting small and large businesses, and through which everyday users in some parts of the world can catch an Uber using a chatbot in WhatsApp, do their shopping, receive business deals and promotions, pay bills and even have their ID and other personal documents verified (Mari, 2020; Soeyuenmez, 2022).[2] Such is the experience of users in India and Brazil, where WhatsApp's business features and other design updates are often first tested before they are rolled out elsewhere.

In tracing these developments, the chapter is divided into three main sections. First, we situate WhatsApp in the context of the 'appification' of global culture (Ling et al., 2020; Morris & Murray, 2018). We use insights from mobile media scholars (Goggin, 2006; Goggin & Hjorth, 2008; Hjorth et al., 2012; Ling & Lai, 2016; Ling et al., 2020) to position WhatsApp within the smartphone revolution, focusing specifically on the emergence of the app store as a key infrastructure facilitating the uptake of mobile instant messaging. In the second section, we describe WhatsApp's origin story and evolution, from 2009 up until its purchase by Meta in 2014. We trace WhatsApp's development from its original design, and the vision of its founders, Koum and Acton, to its evolution in relation to Asian and North American competitors in the messaging ecosystem, providing insight into its similarity to and departure from these technologies and their business models.

The third section focuses on the period following Meta's purchase of WhatsApp. Here, we turn our attention to how Meta sought to leverage WhatsApp's already significant user base to expand its reach in the Global South. We examine how the 'Free Basics' program, pioneered by Meta to increase dependency on its flagship platform, Facebook, was used to grow WhatsApp's user base in the Global South to the extent that for many it became the main access point to the internet

(Bucher, 2021; Gómez Cruz & Harindranath, 2020; Nothias, 2020; Pereira & Bojzuk, 2018). The section concludes by turning to the question many commentators were asking in the early years of Meta's purchase of WhatsApp: how Meta would monetize the app. Tracing this development, we examine one of the many scandals initiated by design and policy changes intended to make the platform profitable, referring to the departure of founders Acton and Koum after Meta introduced changes to its Terms of Service to facilitate business integrations, betraying its earlier promises. This is a defining moment that paved the way for WhatsApp's development into a global communication and business platform. This transformation, we argue, has gradually challenged Acton and Koum's vision of WhatsApp as a privacy-focused, simple and reliable communication tool.

The appification of global culture

Mobile media studies are an important starting point for our analysis, providing a rear-view mirror glance at the development of mobile communication apps, from the introduction of the cell phone to the smartphone revolution and the appification of culture through the Apple iOS store.

Early scholarship on mobile media already observed that mobile phones did more than render telephony mobile by replacing fixed-line, one-to-one calls with those on wireless and mobile networks. They extended the very meaning of telephony by converging telecommunication and software developments, and were generative of new mobile lifestyles and cultures (Hjorth et al., 2012). Texting has been analysed as one example of how users appropriated cell phone technologies and features, such as short messaging service or SMS, to 'tame' or domesticate the technology, shaping unique practices and cultures (Ling, 2010). Further developments in telecommunications and computing paved the way for the launch of the Apple iPhone in 2007, sparking rapid global uptake

(Goggin, 2021). Later, with the launch of the iOS app store, scholars heralded another paradigm shift: the 'appification' of culture (Ling et al., 2020, p. 3; Morris & Murray, 2018). Prior to this time, mobile software applications or 'apps' (Morris & Murray, 2018, p. 4) lived on users' mobile phones in the form of simple programs – like Snake and Tetris, calendar, maps. It was not until the launch of the iOS store, and later Google Play, TenCent, My App and others, that mobile apps came to rival web-based applications and 'crystallise a certain definition of apps that has come to shape how we think of the relationship between software and ourselves' (Morris & Murray, 2018, p. 4).

The launch of the iOS store and software developer kit was especially significant (Goggin, 2021, p. 34), transforming the landscape for developers, who could sell or make their apps available for free download through the store as a distribution 'platform' and marketplace. Through these innovations, smartphones became a gateway to millions of discrete apps that were single function or complex, multifunctional, multimedia ecosystems of their own. The iOS store, in 2008 'debuted with close to 500 apps that garnered over 10 million downloads during its first weekend' (Morris & Murray, 2018, p. 5). WhatsApp, though launching later, in 2009, stands in the rankings as the third most downloaded app of all time (data.ai, 2022). In fact, at the time of writing, three of the top 10 most downloaded apps of all time are messaging apps (Messenger, WhatsApp, Snapchat) underscoring how important they are in the global app ecology. For users, the possibility of making free calls and texts – one-to-one, one-to-many and many-to-many – revolutionized everyday communication. This was particularly so in contexts such as India and Brazil (WhatsApp's largest markets) where poor telecommunications infrastructure and monopolization of telecommunications markets made standard voice calls and SMS unaffordable for ordinary users (Gajjala & Verma, 2018; Saboia, 2016).

WhatsApp co-exists within this app ecosystem with other players including Facebook Messenger, Kik, Snapchat,

WeChat, Telegram, Viber, KakaoTalk and LINE (the latter two are dominant in South Korea and Japan respectively). In a general sense, the increasing numbers of messaging apps since the launch of the iOS Store suggest a complicated array of new developments in private and public communications, including: the increasing importance of private and group chats in everyday life (Chen et al., 2018; Ling & Lai, 2016; Rettberg, 2018), the role of messaging apps as content-sharing platforms, and for commercial and monetary exchanges (Chen et al., 2018; Steinberg, 2020) and in various kinds of political campaigning and mobilization (Kresna, 2018; Sun & Yu, 2020). WhatsApp's story enhances understanding of how Meta's industrial development has been shaped in important ways by the rise of apps, and of mobile messaging specifically, and this is a point that has so far been overlooked in the existing scholarship on both Meta and WhatsApp.

Origins and evolution

WhatsApp is identified as one of the first messaging apps to launch on the Apple iOS store. In an interview in 2014, Acton told readers that he initially left Yahoo to develop WhatsApp because of Yahoo's 'NASCAR approach' of plastering web pages with ad banners (Olson, 2018). Koum likewise saw promise in the app revolution taking shape after the launch of Apple's iOS store (Morris & Murray, 2018), with the growth in mobile apps offering an opportunity to free himself from the commercialized web. Initially, Koum saw a gap for a simple mobile app which could access your phone contact list, allowing you to share status updates with your close friends and family. As recalled in an interview with Koum's friend (and fellow tech entrepreneur) Alex Fishman, 'Jan was showing me his address book ... His thinking was it would be really cool to have statuses next to the individual names of people so you knew what was happening, for example, if they were out and didn't want to be called, or if their battery was dying. Hence the name WhatsApp, or what's up?' (Olson, 2018).

New features were introduced after June 2009, with Apple launching push notifications, meaning WhatsApp users could see a pop-up message on their phone's home screen if a friend's status changed – a feature that helped to ensure constant user engagement. The affordances of the iPhone further aided WhatsApp's technical evolution, transforming it from a basic status update app into an instant messaging application enabling free text-based messages (Santos & Faure, 2018, p. 6). WhatsApp 2.0 (as the Instant Messaging version was called) was launched on Apple iOS store in August 2009, and success quickly followed with the app reaching 250,000 active users by December 2009 (Iqbal, 2022). Acton and Koum sought seed funding from other ex-Yahoo employees, and, in December 2009, WhatsApp launched photo- and video-sharing, presenting itself as not only a free alternative to SMS, but also lauding new multimedia messaging options.

Multimedia and image-sharing features enhanced the social uses of WhatsApp, with photos deepening connections between family, friends and intimate partners. In a blog post in 2014, Koum claimed that in countries where WhatsApp's growth had skyrocketed in the five years since its launch, including Brazil, India, Mexico and Russia, users 'sent more than 700 million photos and 100 million videos every day' (Dredge, 2014). From its humble beginnings, WhatsApp has grown its list of social features and affordances, but its early promise of providing a secure, ad-free way to communicate with family, friends and close acquaintances remained a core promise under Koum and Acton's stewardship. In an interview, Koum distilled the company's philosophy into three core principles: that the service would not carry advertising; it would not store messages on its servers (risking users' privacy); and it would maintain a focus on delivering a 'gimmickless, reliable, friction-free user experience' (Santos & Faure, 2018, p. 9).

There is a variety of reasons for WhatsApp's rapid uptake among different user cohorts around the world, but interviews with users in India have indicated the simplicity of registering via mobile phone 'without the need to "log on" ... with IDs and passwords' is one of them (Gajjala & Verma, 2018, p. 206). Easy-to-use features, such as the ones afforded by WhatsApp, opened up mobile internet to multiple generations in India, Latin America and across the Middle East, shaping 'new forms of co-presence and sociality for transnationally dispersed families' (Wilding et al., 2020, p. 648; see also Alinejad, 2019; Madianou, 2014). It has even been claimed that WhatsApp's entry into Mexico broke down societal divides of class and literacy by allowing multimodal conversations using 'iconic forms such as emojis, stickers, gifs and memes' (Gómez Cruz & Harindranath, 2020). By the end of 2013, WhatsApp had acquired 400 million active users globally, placing it ahead of Facebook Messenger and WeChat as the world's largest messaging app (Statista, 2023).

On the basis of its success, it began receiving acquisition offers from a number of companies, including Google (Rushe, 2014). These offers were initially turned down, and WhatsApp continued introducing new possibilities for connectivity and sociality within the app. These included things such as voice messages, a feature blending the asynchronous capabilities of text with a time-saving and more intimate way of communicating with friends and family that quickly surpassed text messaging in some contexts, as we further unpack in chapter 3. But, while WhatsApp was leading in many markets, the problem of monetizing the app was an underlying issue, with a number of WhatsApp public updates in 2013 speaking of the necessary trade-off of charging a 99¢ yearly subscription fee to allow WhatsApp to operate ad-free. At the same time, the growth of East Asian 'superapps' (primarily WeChat in China and LINE in Japan; Steinberg, 2020), as well as emerging North American rivals (Telegram and Snapchat), had begun to increase competition in global messaging markets.

Competition and the rise of superapps

Between 2010 and 2013, mobile internet and smartphone use overtook fixed line broadband and desktop computers as the main access point to the internet in many markets around the world. In some regions (Asian and African countries notably) this trend was so pronounced that countries, such as India, came to be regarded as mobile-first markets (Statista, 2023). In this context, mobile apps began to transform business practices, media industries and everyday life and culture rapidly. The global adoption of the iPhone – converging internet, telephony and software – combined with strong support from government policies, led East Asian software developers to create products for mobile rather than adapting web-based software applications. KakaoTalk, LINE and WeChat emerged in this context, competing directly against WhatsApp in domestic and global markets.

KakaoTalk was the first, launched in 2009, the same year as WhatsApp. Initially the developers used WhatsApp as the developmental benchmark (Choi, 2013) but several innovative features represented a departure from WhatsApp; specifically, it had an e-commerce feature which allowed friends to buy and send gifts to each other via text message (Jin & Yoon, 2016). The integration of KakaoTalk with popular games such as *Anipang* also brought messaging and gaming industries together, making it a leader in the reorientation of smartphone and messenger cultures away from text and talk towards 'play' (Jin & Yoon, 2016, p. 514). This was a first step in transforming messaging apps into mobile media platforms (Nieborg & Helmond, 2019; Steinberg, 2020). Opposing this integration of gaming, WhatsApp's founders instead integrated features that transformed how people consumed news and ran their business, as we will explore in chapters 2–5.

South Korean messaging app, LINE, developed by internet search giant, Naver (Steinberg, 2020) was launched in 2011 in the Japanese market, given the difficulty of competing against KakaoTalk in South Korea (Jin & Yoon, 2016). Unlike WhatsApp and KakaoTalk, LINE pursued a business strategy of 'platformization' from the outset (Nieborg & Helmond, 2019) with its ambition to transform LINE into a 'Swiss army knife', with a host of add-on apps layered on top of its core messaging function (Steinberg, 2020, p. 1). Text messaging and calls have always been free on LINE, but one year after launch, Naver announced that it would be adding more paid services in the form of cultural content (stickers) and a digital currency for LINE users, called LINE coins – similar to KakaoTalk digital money (Steinberg, 2020, p. 4). By 2016, LINE connected users to 35 paid apps offering services ranging from news aggregation, travel booking, music streaming, shopping, food delivery, taxi hailing, job searching, a live self-broadcasting video, as well as links to LINE published and branded games (Steinberg, 2020, p. 4). The commercial decision to make the core communication app the gateway to these other apps quickly made LINE one of the most profitable platforms on the planet, and a forerunner to the 'superapp' model. In 2014, the year Meta purchased WhatsApp, LINE reported a gross revenue of $656 million (Horwitz, 2015). In the same year, WhatsApp earned only $20 million (Olson, 2014).

As one of the first Asian superapps, LINE had a considerable influence on WhatsApp's own 'platformization' which we focus on in chapter 2. Nonetheless, WhatsApp's closest rival in the messaging landscape, in terms of active users (even though the user base remains predominantly China-based), is WeChat, launched in 2011. Owned and developed by China's largest and most successful tech company, TenCent, when WeChat launched, promotional material described it as the 'least data consuming cell phone walkie talkie' on the market (Chen et al., 2018, pp. 3, 7). It was soon compared to WhatsApp (p. 3), whose low data usage model had made it popular in global markets. The Chinese government strongly supported WeChat, with public Official Accounts being established to streamline government communications between the Communist Party of China (CPC), Chinese citizens and the global Chinese diaspora, paving the way for WeChat to become a communications infrastructure for business and government (pp. 38–9). The growth of a range of social and commercial features, combined with government support, fashioned WeChat into more than an app. It became a public communication platform that is now integrated into, and shapes, private, business, cultural and government communications, commercial transactions and whole industries in China (Brunton, 2018).

Steinberg (2020) and Goggin (2021) use the term 'superapp' to describe KakaoTalk, LINE and WeChat's development into a 'platform to support all platforms' (Steinberg, 2020, p. 1). The term has grown in usage among mobile media and platform scholars focused on Asian digital markets, with 'superapp' being used to mark a divergence from the previously dominant Silicon Valley 'platform' model. In the latter, platforms use a number of web and app 'instances' (Nieborg & Helmond, 2019) to reach out into the web and mobile ecosystem, and draw data back into their 'data-gathering ecosystem' (Nieborg & Helmond, 2019, p. 4), while extracting and transforming personal user data into a commodity to be sold to advertisers and businesses. By contrast, superapps (and the mega-corporations behind them) aim to create interdependencies between users, labour, businesses and financial providers, and monetize this data traffic – all within the boundaries of a single app interface (Steinberg et al., 2022, p. 1407). This consolidates media power in one app.

WhatsApp follows some aspects of this trend touted as a 'next phase in the digital economy' (Goggin, 2021, p. 74), but departs in some key aspects as well, which we articulate further in chapters 2 and 5. In pinpointing how superapps came to 'rule them all' (Chen et al., 2018) in the East Asian context, scholars have noted the way they solved the monetization problem by more effectively integrating an array of services with 'backend payment, digital, mobile money and fin-tech systems' (Goggin, 2021, p. 75). Many consider WeChat to be the pinnacle of the superapp model (Chen et al., 2018) by virtue of its evolution into a technology that offers opportunities for everyday users to be connected to employers, business clients, advertisers, brands and government services, all in one place.

Presenting a different narrative to the rise of the superapp in East Asia, North American messaging apps such as WhatsApp, Messenger and Snapchat initially offered simplicity, with their original design being oriented towards private chat. This design choice offered something different to the broadcast style communication of social media platforms like Facebook and Twitter, and the Asian superapp model which transformed mobile communication apps into a marketplace or 'bazaar' for cultural and commercial products and services (Chen et al., 2018, p. 16).

Tracking this alternative development pathway, WhatsApp's cousin, Messenger, was developed in 2008, before the smartphone app revolution even began. It was originally integrated with Facebook to enable instant messaging between users of the platform (Gangneux, 2021). This limited its appeal, given that users had to create a Facebook account to use it (Gajjala & Verma, 2018). However, Messenger was disaggregated from the mother platform in 2011, and launched on Apple iOS store as a standalone, cross-platform instant messaging application (Nieborg & Helmond, 2019). It was gradually upgraded between 2011 and 2013 with the common array of features available on other messaging apps, including group chats, audio and video calls (including group calls). Other features facilitated the sharing of popular cultural forms (stickers, gifs, video, news articles) and allowed users to react to individual messages. In North American markets, Messenger was more popular than WhatsApp which, though developed by Silicon Valley entrepreneurs, had at this time gained wider appeal in Europe (Germany and Spain primarily), India, South America and Africa. Though developed as a private chat app, Messenger did eventually go through a process of 'platformization' – as indicated in the Introduction (Nieborg & Helmond, 2019) – foreshadowing WhatsApp's own evolution into a communication and business platform as we will explore in later chapters.

Snapchat is another success story of the Silicon Valley messaging apps. A year after its launch, in 2011, Snapchat reached 10 million users, becoming a youth cultural force (Rettberg, 2018). Snapchat's appeal to younger audiences related to a feature that separated it from other social media platforms and chatting apps, with users being able to share self-timed (1–10 seconds) disappearing images (or 'snaps') to their friends. This prompted users to share in the moment, mundane 'snaps' that captured the fleeting nature of everyday life (Rettberg, 2018, p. 191). The positive response to this shift had a strong influence on the subsequent development of Silicon Valley messaging apps, with both Messenger and WhatsApp introducing features that allowed for ephemeral media, carrying on the privacy and security-focused design of North American apps.

Telegram, created by Russian entrepreneur, Pavel Durov, entered the increasingly competitive global messaging market in 2013 with a cloud-based platform that encrypted messages between phone and server, and also incorporated end-to-end encryption as an opt-in feature for one-to-one chats, providing a shield against government surveillance (Santos & Faure, 2018; Santos et al., 2021). The app quickly became popular with activists and citizens staring down authoritarian governments in Brazil, Turkey, India, the UK and parts of Southeast Asia (Johns, 2020; Santos et al., 2021) – markets in which

WhatsApp also dominated. In fact, Telegram's emergence in these markets may have had some influence on WhatsApp's decision to roll out end-to-end encryption in 2016, given that WhatsApp and Telegram have continued, in the intervening years, to trade barbs concerning which platform is more secure or has the most fail-safe encryption (Loucaides, 2023). The encryption feature will be discussed in more detail in chapters 2 and 4 where the appeal of encrypted messaging to activists will be a point of focus.

This evolution of messaging apps provides an important context for the story we tell of WhatsApp's development, demonstrating some key differences between North American messaging apps (including WhatsApp at this stage of its development) and the 'superapp' model of East Asian platforms LINE, KakaoTalk and WeChat. Technically, while the superapp model offered users an array of integrated services, including economic transactions, all in one place, North American messaging apps' decision to promote 'privacy' and 'simplicity' as their core selling point challenged monetization options. This saw many of the superapps generate large profits by comparison to Silicon Valley rivals such as WhatsApp, which was still predominantly focused on building a private and simple service for interpersonal communication. Although businesses in countries such as Brazil and India had already started using WhatsApp as an informal marketplace where they could sell their products and communicate with customers, as we explore further in chapters 2 and 5, this had not yet become a formal aspect of WhatsApp's design. Tellingly, Koum and Acton boasted at the time of Meta's purchase that the reason WhatsApp was more globally popular than LINE and KakaoTalk was precisely because WhatsApp was not 'bloated' from adding games, music, shopping and other commercially driven features which they claimed made for a 'shitty' user experience (Dredge, 2014). However, their tone did shift after partnering with Meta, as we explore next.

After Meta

When Meta purchased WhatsApp for $19 billion in 2014, the price tag shocked observers. The largest amount Meta had previously paid for a tech acquisition was $1 billion, for Instagram in 2012. The massive investment in WhatsApp was easier to understand, however, in the context of Meta's ambitions to make its business mobile-first (Bucher, 2021; Goggin, 2021) following the enormous growth of mobile instant messaging in emerging, untapped markets. At the time of the purchase, WhatsApp was growing at a rate of 1 million users per day (Deutsch et al., 2022), with the greatest proportion of new users being located in the emerging markets of India and Brazil. In those markets, WhatsApp was fast outpacing Facebook Messenger and even catching up to Meta's flagship platform, Facebook (Warzel & Mac, 2018). By purchasing WhatsApp, Meta was joining forces with its biggest rival in mobile messaging, essentially killing off its major competition. It also now had a horse in a race being defined by the East Asian superapps at this time, but which Meta would soon redefine with its own unique blueprint for growing WhatsApp into a global communication and business platform.

Free Basics and digital colonialism

India, Brazil and other emerging economies in the Global South have been key to Meta's vision for economic growth since Meta purchased WhatsApp. One very controversial aspect of this focus has been the expansion of 'Free Basics' to include WhatsApp. Free Basics is the name of a Meta initiative introduced in 2013, one year before Meta purchased WhatsApp. The program revolved around a data-lite, text-based version of Facebook which was bundled with other websites and news services, and made available for free through users' data plans. Meta targeted Free Basics at consumers in the Global

South, where poor infrastructure and expensive data plans meant that accessing data-consuming services like Facebook was virtually impossible. To lower barriers, Meta made deals with local telecoms to 'zero-rate'[3] Free Basics, onboarding potentially millions of new customers lured by the promise of free internet and texting.

Free Basics was launched with the promise to 'connect the next billion' to Meta's core commercial product, Facebook (Bucher, 2021, p. 131; Nothias, 2020). In promotional speeches, Mark Zuckerberg described Free Basics as a key driver of Meta's philanthropic vision to close the 'digital divide', eventually bringing online the world's estimated 5 billion users without internet access (Nothias, 2020). To put this into context, it is reported that mobile data plans to this day (and certainly in 2014) cost the average user in these markets a high percentage of their monthly income, making calls, messaging and access to basic internet services barely affordable (Wodinsky, 2021). One reason for this disparity was lax regulation of the telecommunications sector, which had allowed companies to form monopolies, pricing some users out of the market. In Brazil, for example, the cost of texting using SMS was '55 times more expensive than in North America' (Saboia, 2016).

While 'Free Basics' was Meta's entry point into these markets, WhatsApp (then owned by Koum and Acton) was a direct competitor. WhatsApp already offered a data-lite service that allowed users to text for free as long as people had a 'cheap device and some sort of internet connection' (Wodinsky, 2021). This made connecting with family and friends affordable for the first time, and people took to WhatsApp in large numbers (Gómez Cruz & Harindranath, 2020). Realizing that the entry of technologies like WhatsApp would impact profits, network operators started to zero-rate these services in the hope that users would eventually pay for data (Nothias, 2020, p. 332). In Mexico, where WhatsApp was already popular, the introduction of plans which zero-rated

WhatsApp data meant that most mobile users invested 'just enough funds to have a WhatsApp for free bundle', making WhatsApp 'synonymous with mobile communication' (Gómez Cruz & Harindranath, 2020). Meta's Free Basics program, when first launched, helped to onboard customers to Facebook. But WhatsApp threatened the take-up of Free Basics. It already offered a low data alternative to Facebook and Meta's own mobile product, Messenger, which was lagging behind WhatsApp. This presented a strong business case for Meta to purchase WhatsApp. Documents obtained by journalists from a British Parliamentary Committee hearing in 2018 (Warzel & Mac, 2018) reveal that Meta had been 'obsessively tracking' WhatsApp's growth prior to its eventual offer, using data provided by analytics firm Onavo (which Meta also later purchased in 2013). The data painted a clear picture of WhatsApp's growth and Messenger's decline in both US and emerging markets.

After purchasing WhatsApp, Meta strongly targeted Brazil, India and numerous countries in Africa for the rollout of Free Basics (Nothias, 2020), with WhatsApp added to the bundle. The company's aggressive strategy in Brazil is considered a key reason why the country got to the point where WhatsApp, or *Zap Zap* as it is popularly known (Pereira & Bojzuk, 2018) became the default platform for communicating and receiving news for 96 per cent of the population (Saboia, 2016). Media scholars have addressed zero-rating as a 'harmful business practice', which made Facebook and WhatsApp not just an access point for the internet, but *the internet* in Brazil, 'especially for the most vulnerable communities' (Casaes & Córdova, 2019, p. 4). For Meta, the profile of these countries – very large populations, low rates of internet access, high rates of mobile consumption, and, as discussed, lack of regulatory oversight – made them 'ideal testing grounds for data extraction and technological experiments' (Nothias, 2020, p. 331).

In a keynote speech to 2014's World Mobile Congress, Zuckerberg claimed that the acquisition of WhatsApp was intimately linked to his plans for 'Free Basics'. While he continued to frame Free Basics as part of a humanitarian mission which gave internet access to the unconnected, at the same time, Zuckerberg put his business case to the mobile network operators in attendance – Free Basics would drive economic growth for their companies (Nothias, 2020, p. 332). This also stands as the blueprint for Meta's own commercial ambitions for Free Basics and WhatsApp in Global South countries, which is to make Meta the entry point or 'on-ramp' for the internet (Global Voices, 2017). As Bucher (2021) argues, Free Basics carried on from other similar business ventures for Meta where 'connecting the whole world meant entering into strategic partnerships with mobile network operators and equipment manufacturers' to build the infrastructure for Meta's platforms in the Global South (p. 131). While the opportunities for users to access content and services via Free Basics was limited, for Meta the opportunity to create dependencies on its services was huge, and a vital part of its business plan: 'access for all in this case means … a business opportunity worth five billion eyeballs' (Bucher, 2021, p. 133).

But the Free Basics program was by no means without its detractors. From the very beginning, the program had attracted strong criticism from human rights organizations, and eventually regulators, who claimed that the company was not being altruistic but was instead creating a 'walled garden' in which to trap users (Nothias, 2020, p. 330). These objections emerged most explosively in India, where the telecommunications regulator, TRAI, banned Free Basics in 2016 after massive online protests by an activist group called Save the Internet (STI). Meta had set its sight on India as a prime site for rolling out Free Basics owing to the country's digital footprint (only 15 per cent of the country's large and growing population was online in 2013) and the massive uptake of WhatsApp in the country. In 2014 a Free Basics summit was held in India and attended by Prime Minister

Modi. A few months afterwards, Meta announced Free Basics would be rolling out in six Indian states. But rather than welcoming the program, STI launched a year-long campaign that drew worldwide attention, and sparked heated debate about whether Free Basics contravened important principles of 'net neutrality'[4] (Global Voices, 2017). The activists, who mainly hailed from the tech sector and media industries, claimed that schemes like Free Basics locked users into a narrow range of content governed by a small number of powerful companies, and stamped out competition from smaller players. This led to the scheme being referred to as a type of 'digital colonialism' (Bucher, 2021; Solon, 2017). The activists' campaign pressured TRAI to act, leading to its eventual ban in what has been described as Meta's 'first major political scandal on the global stage' (Nothias, 2020, p. 330).

In response to the Indian ban, Meta CEO Mark Zuckerberg wrote an op-ed piece in *The Times of India* where he argued that claims of digital colonialism were 'fiction' and instead Free Basics extended Meta's plans to 'connect the world' and narrow the digital divide (Zuckerberg, 2015): 'Instead of wanting to give people access to some basic internet services for free, critics of the program continue to spread false claims – even if that means leaving behind a billion people', he wrote, adding: 'Who could possibly be against this?' This was followed by a study conducted by Global Voices in 2017, where researchers who downloaded the Free Basics app found that, apart from violating principles of net neutrality, it granted Meta access to 'unique streams of data about the habits and interests of users in developing countries' (Global Voices, 2017).

While this very public campaign against Free Basics led to the service being banned in India, in Africa, critical voices were fewer in number and Meta's plans continued relatively unhindered, such that in 2019 Free Basics was still quietly available in 28 African countries, making Facebook and WhatsApp the default gateway to the internet in these countries (Nothias, 2020, p. 335). For scholars inquiring into this discrepancy, it was revealed that Facebook's strategy to capture markets in Africa evolved as a result of the stand-off with civil society groups and regulators in India. In Africa, Meta engaged more strongly with local civil society organizations and activists, re-focusing digital rights campaigns on government censorship and efforts to shut down the internet, which were often greater, existential concerns to activists than net neutrality or anti-competitive practices by social media platforms. Organizations that Meta invested in included data journalism and civic tech organizations, children's rights and digital literacy organizations, and fact-checking organizations such as Africa Check.

The investment in fact-checking organizations in Africa ironically coincided with criticisms levelled at Free Basics in countries like Brazil and the Philippines, where the program was claimed to foster the spread of misinformation. This was related to the fact it locked users in, and they could only access a limited number of sources on the internet. Critics argue that this has contributed to a rising tide of misinformation circulating on WhatsApp, particularly for the poorest users dependent on Free Basics. Journalists and researchers from Brazil regard zero-rating practices as one reason why pseudo-scientific health information and conspiracy theories went viral on WhatsApp during the Zika virus and COVID-19 pandemic, undermining public health promotion of vaccines (Casaes & Córdova, 2019). It has also been considered critical to Jair Bolsonaro's poisoning of WhatsApp groups in the lead up to the 2018 Presidential election in Brazil (Lorenzon, 2021), with the circulation of audios and images containing misinformation being the only media diet some users were exposed to, as will be further explored in chapters 2 and 4. But while its colonization of markets in the Global South helped to develop WhatsApp as a gateway service and 'infrastructure', it still did not solve the problem of how to monetize the app. The next stage of WhatsApp's evolution addressed this problem, transforming WhatsApp into a *business* platform.

The monetization question

Between 2014 and 2017, press coverage revealed intense speculation around how Meta intended to monetize WhatsApp. The company was still run by Koum – who had been made CEO, as part of the deal with Meta – while Acton maintained a large stake in the company. As the founders had long maintained that ads would never be introduced to WhatsApp, the purchase by Meta, an ad-driven company, raised eyebrows. To reassure users, Acton and Koum explained after the sale that a key part of the deal was a promise from Mark Zuckerberg that WhatsApp would remain independent, that monetization plans would be frozen for at least 5 years and that ads would never be part of the strategy (Olson, 2018; Yarow, 2014). This was important to Koum and Acton, whose promise of 'no ads' was a pledge they had made to users since the beginning, and to which they remained committed after the sale to Meta. Their first blog post after the sale read:

> Today we are announcing a partnership with Facebook ... WhatsApp will remain autonomous and operate independently. You can continue to enjoy the service for a nominal fee. You can continue to use WhatsApp no matter where in the world you are, or what smartphone you're using. And you can still count on absolutely no ads interrupting your communication. There would have been no partnership between our two companies if we had to compromise on the core principles that will always define our company, our vision and our product.[5]

Despite these promises, media commentators were sceptical that Meta would keep its promise for long. Some pondered whether the pledge to remain ad free would hold (Chawla, 2014; Garner, 2015). Others, including Kik CEO, Ted Livingstone, viewed future monetization strategies from the perspective of how WhatsApp would be able to stay relevant in markets where it competed directly against the superapps, which had developed into platforms where users could pay for services using in-app digital money (Chawla, 2014; Livingstone 2014).

In 2016, it seemed that things were changing in the relationship between Meta and WhatsApp with Koum announcing on the company blog that WhatsApp would be dropping the paid subscription model and looking at other revenue opportunities. Koum assured users that this would not see 'banner' advertising on WhatsApp, but that the company would instead seek to leverage the organic connections businesses had built up with clients on WhatsApp in markets like Brazil (Saboia, 2016) and India (Babu, 2016; Mehta, 2015). An article published after Koum's announcement brought up the 'superapp' question again, with business analysts reflecting on whether WhatsApp would be trying to emulate WeChat, becoming a platform for other developers to build services on top of:

> In industry parlance, this is known as moving from a service to a 'platform'; becoming a base on which software developers can build their own services ... In aiming to become platforms, WhatsApp and Facebook Messenger have been inspired by the success of WeChat, a Chinese app owned by internet giant Tencent. While China's citizens use WeChat to talk to family and friends, they also use it to pay bills, make medical appointments, and check traffic. (Titcomb, 2016)

While superapp comparisons continued to dominate press headlines, particularly in WhatsApp's key markets, another detail that was shared in a 2016 blog post signalled other ways that WhatsApp could drive Meta's advertising business. The post provided insight into how extracting data from WhatsApp could be used to personalize ads on Facebook:

> By coordinating more with Facebook, we'll be able to do things like track basic metrics about how often people use our services and better fight spam on WhatsApp. And by connecting your phone number with Facebook's systems, Facebook can offer better friend suggestions and show you more relevant ads if you have an account with them.[6]

The vision, which seemed to fly in the face of the founders' earlier promises, was further expanded in Meta's Q2 2017 earnings call (Meta Platforms, Inc., 2017), where Zuckerberg and CFO David Wehner reflected on new revenue streams that they envisioned for WhatsApp. In the call, they discussed the similar business strategies that Meta was pursuing for its two mobile assets, WhatsApp and Messenger. Zuckerberg announced that the company would be seeking to 'build a business ecosystem' around both messaging apps. But, whereas Messenger was in more advanced stages of opening up to third-party developers and advertisers, Wehner explained that WhatsApp's development was still in a pre-monetization phase:

> We're focused on growing the user base, first and foremost. And then secondly, it's about building organic connections between businesses and consumers. And then third, it's about how do we build monetization around those relationships ... And I think there, we're further along with Messenger than we are with WhatsApp. David Wehner, quoted in Larkin (2017)

This laid out a flexible business plan for turning WhatsApp into a platform following similar changes to Messenger. Importantly, the call mimicked the steps of 'platformization' described by Nieborg and Helmond (2019, p. 207) in their investigation into Messenger's transformation, as detailed in the Introduction. They describe this as a three-step model of (1) building the app into a 'ubiquitous utility' for around 1–2 billion users, (2) evolving the platform into a multi-sided market where businesses and advertisers can interact with users, and (3) 'monetization' which, in most cases, means 'dialing up advertising'.

Meanwhile, behind closed doors, an exclusive interview with Brian Acton in 2018 (Olson, 2018) revealed that pressure from Meta to lay the groundwork for data sharing between WhatsApp and Meta had commenced before the 2014 deal had even gone through. Acton recalled that Meta executives coached Koum and Acton on how to reassure representatives of the European Competition Commission – who were scrutinizing the deal from the perspective of European antitrust laws – that it would be impossible to 'blend' data between Meta's systems and WhatsApp. At the same time Meta was secretly developing technologies to do precisely this. Eighteen months later, the announcement that privacy updates would be introduced to allow greater data sharing between WhatsApp and Meta came to pass. As Acton claims, this change was a 'crucial first step toward monetization' which the founders 'pushed back' against, fearing that it would open the doorway for businesses to be able to engage in direct marketing to WhatsApp users.

Acton, who would leave WhatsApp in 2018, later claimed that the final straw was a meeting in which Zuckerberg laid out a plan for showing ads in WhatsApp's status feature. This was coupled with plans to sell tools which would enable businesses to chat with customers, and, eventually, provide them with user analytics. The flaw in the plan was the end-to-end encryption that Koum and Acton had designed with the blessing of Meta, and which had been used by Meta to help restore its reputation in key markets after privacy breaches. Despite public statements that encryption was central to Meta's vision for WhatsApp, Acton claimed that, behind the scenes, Meta executives were continuously trying to find ways to share user data with businesses 'in an encrypted environment' to shore up its business strategy (Olson, 2018). Acton opted to leave WhatsApp later that year to start up encryption and privacy-focused non-profit, Signal Foundation.[7] He later became a vocal critic of Meta (Facebook), advising his many followers on Twitter: 'It's time #deleteFacebook'. Koum followed suit in 2018, with both departures removing any obstacles in the way of Meta's plan to develop WhatsApp into a business platform.

WhatsApp's unique trajectory of platformization – and appropriation and resistance toward this vision from users, regulators and governments – will be discussed in more detail in chapter 2. In this chapter we have laid the foundation for our argument that WhatsApp is no longer a simple communication app, but has transformed into a global communication and business platform – a platform where users run their businesses and communicate with brands and advertisers, receive communications from the government and, at the same time, enjoy intimate communications with family and friends. In blending all these experiences together, WhatsApp has become 'sticky', making users unlikely to leave even if they disagree with certain business decisions and design choices. At the same time, we have also highlighted how regulators, human rights organizations and privacy advocates have sometimes challenged Meta's efforts to monetize WhatsApp by developing it as a hybrid space blending private and public chat, and this draws attention to the contestations implicit in WhatsApp's ongoing transformation.

Conclusion

In this chapter, we have examined WhatsApp's evolution from a simple chatting app into a business and communication platform by reflecting on three phases of its development. In the first section, we have situated the development of WhatsApp's key features in the context of 'the smartphone revolution' and the emergence of the app store as a key technology that gave rise to mobile instant messaging. The second section has focused on WhatsApp's origin story. Created by two ex-Yahoo employees, the founding vision of WhatsApp was to create a simple status update app which would have 'no ads, no games, no gimmicks', and would instead cater to users' more simple needs for social connection. We have explained how WhatsApp grew in popularity in the Global South as a result of its simple, low data-usage design, which appealed to users in contexts where paying for mobile data was too expensive for many. As a result, WhatsApp became 'sticky' to users' everyday communication needs, leading WhatsApp to rapidly become more than a chatting app. Instead, in key markets it has been described as a 'technology for life', which users cannot leave because all their networks are stored on it, and many of their daily needs are met through it.

We have located WhatsApp's early development in the context of a global instant messaging ecosystem. This particular context shaped WhatsApp's evolution in certain ways as it evolved in competition with rival messaging apps and their different design choices and business models. The chapter has highlighted a divergence in the global messaging landscape between East Asian 'superapps' (WeChat, KakaoTalk and LINE), and North American and Russian-owned privacy-focused apps (Messenger, Snapchat, Telegram and others), and finds, in these tensions, different pathways that have influenced WhatsApp's development. We have sought to understand how East Asian superapps have influenced WhatsApp's platformization. Scholarship has shown how East Asian superapps became the first messaging apps to 'platformize', opposing the privacy focus of North American and Russian-owned apps. The superapps allowed developers to build services and experiences on top of their core communication apps, while also providing backend e-commerce and digital payment systems so that services can be paid for in-app. This integration of all users' needs in one place is important to WhatsApp's story because it showed Meta what WhatsApp could become, and provided an impetus for its purchase in 2014. Although privacy was foregrounded as a core value when encryption was introduced in 2016, the superapp model has also crucially informed the evolution of WhatsApp's business model under Meta, as evident in the recent development of in-app shopping and in-app payments, which we describe in detail in chapter 5.

In the final section, we have examined developments in the years immediately following Meta's purchase of WhatsApp, identifying controversial decisions and design changes which signalled Meta's intention to monetize the app. Meta initially sought to appease Koum and Acton's vision for keeping WhatsApp ad-free and focused on ordinary user needs, but we have charted two steps that departed from this vision, and foreshadowed WhatsApp's transformation in its economic, technological and social dimensions. First, WhatsApp's inclusion in the Free Basics program enabled it to monopolize key markets in the Global South, and increased dependency on WhatsApp as a gateway to the internet for many people. Second, changes to WhatsApp's data-sharing policy paved the way for the evolution of WhatsApp's business features and platformization (examined in closer detail in chapters 2 and 5). These changes undermine Koum and Acton's vision of a simple, ad-free user experience, bringing Meta into confrontation with the founders themselves, regulators and users around the world.

To conclude, WhatsApp matters because of the importance Meta has attributed to it as a key focus of its commercial strategy for economic growth and platform power. But WhatsApp's evolution cannot be fully grasped through reference to this strategy alone. WhatsApp would not have become the world's leading messaging platform had it not been enthusiastically taken up, negotiated and contested by users around the world. It is precisely these negotiations and contestations – the mutual shaping of the technology and user preferences and needs – that have afforded WhatsApp its global reach and 'stickiness', as we explore further in chapter 2.

2

Platform Biography

What is going on with WhatsApp? This is a question that some commentators were posing[1] in 2021 when it was evident that WhatsApp was evolving into a key tool for business. But WhatsApp started transitioning as a platform in its technical, social and economic dimensions much earlier than this. Its emergence as a global communication and business platform was iterative, as WhatsApp progressively changed its design to respond to the way people used it in key markets. The demands of 'exquisitely Indian socializing', for example, led to calls for groups with more than 50 participants in 2014 (Jain, 2014) and WhatsApp now affords groups of thousands of people. Groups are no longer just private spaces for intimate connections; they also mediate new forms of collective life among strangers, similar to open platforms. When journalists and media organizations were grappling with the fact that news was going mobile (Goggin et al., 2015; Wei, 2008), WhatsApp launched the Broadcast list tool to help them reach out to audiences. The feature allowed WhatsApp users, including news organizations, to 'broadcast' messages to many people at once. These examples show that WhatsApp is a technology for more than just communicating privately with friends and family. The process by which platforms and people's uses continually shape and influence each other (Bucher, 2012; Burgess & Baym, 2020; Gillespie, 2018) matters to understand WhatsApp as a platform.

This chapter focuses on the technical evolution of WhatsApp as a platform, and how this technological transformation has always been tested, negotiated and contested by its user base. Drawing on platform studies scholars' suggestion to focus on key technological features as proxies to understand platforms' evolution over time (Bucher, 2012; Burgess & Baym, 2020; van Dijck & Poell, 2013), the chapter focuses on WhatsApp's design elements that are 'keys to participation on the platform' (Burgess & Baym, 2020, p. 35). We take inspiration from Burgess and Baym's (2020) method in their 'biography' of Twitter, in which its main technical features are used as an entry point to examining the specific possibilities and constraints this platform offers to diverse end-users, and the actual practices of use arising from people's appropriation of these features in everyday life.

Burgess and Baym (2020) organize their platform biography in four stages to explain how people take up, use and negotiate Twitter's technical features: appropriation, incorporation, contestation and iteration. They define 'appropriation' as the stage whereby users started using key features on Twitter, such as the hashtag (#), the @mention,[2] and the retweet (RT), long before Twitter formally incorporated these features into its design: what they call the 'incorporation' phase. They use the 'contestation' stage to refer to the period in which users challenge Twitter's design updates, and the 'iteration' stage discusses how the platform further refines its features as a result of a process of negotiation with its users (p. 36). We take a less prescriptive formula to write our platform biography. This means that instead of clearly demarcating different stages in how people use and negotiate WhatsApp's key technical features, we provide short summaries of when these features were introduced by WhatsApp, why they are important for understanding WhatsApp as a platform and how users have contributed to their evolution.

Although the chapter is organized around WhatsApp's design, it is narrated in a way that always considers user agency in WhatsApp's technical development. The chapter is structured into three main sections: Intimacy and privacy-oriented features (including the Group feature, Communities and encryption); broadcast and shareability features (including sharing plug-ins, the Forward feature, and the Broadcast list); and business-oriented features (including the Business App and API). We acknowledge that WhatsApp's main technical features defy easy compartmentalization: for example, the Business App shares end-to-end encryption with WhatsApp's core mobile communication app and businesses can use it to communicate intimately with clients. However, we structure the chapter in these three main sections to facilitate an easy transition to the following chapters in which we delve in more detail into the social dynamics and practices of WhatsApp use in everyday life (chapter 3), in public life (chapter 4), and in its economic dimensions (chapter 5), all of which help us narrate the story of WhatsApp as a platform.

Intimacy and 'privacy-oriented' features

Most literature on WhatsApp conceptualizes this technology as an app for private communication (Church & de Oliveira, 2013; Goggin, 2021; Ling & Lai, 2016). It was originally developed as a technology for personal connection and chat among friends and family and, unlike other more public-facing social media platforms such as Twitter and Facebook, was not extracting user data to predict behaviour and sell ads to people.[3] The Group feature was part of this vision of connecting people 'privately', though its introduction in 2011 also marked the beginning of WhatsApp's transformation from a one-to-one messaging tool (Ling & Lai, 2016) to a global communication platform. The Group feature made WhatsApp more like a social network rather than just a text messaging or voice call service and, as people used it to communicate in and through groups, WhatsApp gave rise to new kinds of collective life and sociability (Pereira & Bojzuk, 2018).

Encryption is another technical feature that contributes to the perception that WhatsApp is a technology for private and personal communication. Since end-to-end encryption deters WhatsApp and third parties from accessing the content that individuals share, it might seem that the feature works against our argument that WhatsApp is a platform. Technically, encryption might seem to limit WhatsApp's ability to process user data for profit, a key component of platforms (Gillespie, 2018; van Dijck & Poell, 2013). It might also seem to limit content moderation, which is also an 'essential, constitutional, definitional' element of platforms, where platforms use tools to 'detect, review' and, if necessary, remove content that goes against its terms of use (Gillespie, 2018, p. 21). However, we argue that end-to-end encryption is key to understanding WhatsApp as a platform. By incorporating this gold standard guarantee of private and secure chat, it effectively hides the other privacy and security vulnerabilities involved in WhatsApp's platformization (Santos & Faure, 2018). WhatsApp does access user data despite encryption, especially since it started developing business-oriented features. It also moderates content despite encryption (Gillespie et al., 2020), and shares user data with third parties (Elkind et al., 2021). In what follows we further unpack how the technical development of the Group feature and encryption, and users' contribution to it, help us conceptualize WhatsApp as a platform.

The Group feature

WhatsApp founders Jan Koum and Brian Acton introduced Group chat for up to five people in 2011 after the community had been asking for this feature for some time.[4] In the beginning, the Group feature was envisioned as a way to extend friend and family connections. As these social networks were small, Koum and Acton saw the Group feature as a way for bringing together people that already knew each other offline. Anyone who had your phone number could add you into a group, and people rapidly found themselves being part of multiple groups. As socialities arising on the app far exceeded the original five-person cap, between 2011 and 2014, WhatsApp progressively increased the group limit in subsequent updates to 15, 50 and then 100 users (Jain, 2014). These redesigns satisfied the needs of its users in key markets such as Southeast Asia, Africa, Latin America and WhatsApp's largest market, India. Although the average WhatsApp group has fewer than ten people (Lu, 2019), research suggests that in countries like Brazil and India these numbers are much higher (Banaji et al., 2019; Caetano et al., 2018).

Communication within groups takes place among close ties as well as looser acquaintances. Examples noted in the literature are leisure-based groups such as sports clubs (Ling & Lai, 2016; Matassi et al., 2019; Swart et al., 2019), educational settings (Ahad & Lim, 2014; Cronje & Zyl, 2022; Dahya et al., 2019; Al Zidjaly, 2014), neighbourhood and other location-based groups (Swart et al., 2019), workplaces (Gómez Cruz & Harindrinath, 2020; Matassi et al., 2019; Pang & Woo, 2020; Swart et al., 2019) and political interest groups (Caetano et al., 2018). There are also important cultural differences in how people use groups and what they expect from this feature too. In countries like Brazil, public groups are common and people use them as online forums to discuss a large array of topics (Caetano et al., 2018; Casaes & Córdova, 2019). Anyone can join a public group as long as they have the link, which is easily searchable on the open web (Casaes & Córdova, 2019, p. 6), constituting WhatsApp as a public forum or open platform.

Indeed, WhatsApp says that one of the 'top requests' they receive is the option to add more people to a group chat,[5] and the feature has technically evolved to satisfy this need. As of February 2023, groups can accommodate up to 1,024 people. But not all users are happy with groups becoming increasingly bigger. When group member limits increased to 256 users in 2016, many people found themselves being added to groups where they did not always know all participants. Some of the WhatsApp users Ariadna interviewed in Barcelona commented on these issues as one of the nuisances of this technology. Jordi, for example, explained this through his own experience:

> **Jordi:** One day a good friend of mine added me to a group where people discuss Catalan politics.
> **Ariadna:** And how many people do you know in this group?
> **Jordi:** Only the friend that added me. One day I shared some content and people asked: 'who is this guy?'
> **Ariadna:** And what topics were discussed in this group?
> **Jordi:** Mainly things about the Independence process in Catalonia. But they sent messages every day without any coherent criteria. It's terrible the amount of nonsense that people share.
>
> Jordi, Barcelona, 2019

As groups got bigger and communication within them more convoluted, the figure of the group admin became key in managing these 'semi-public' communications (Gil de Zúñiga et al., 2021). Within WhatsApp groups, the admin has special controls: they are the ones that can add people to a group, assign 'admin' status to other group members, set group permissions so that only admins are able to send messages and share public group links on the open web. Admins, who are typically the ones that create a group, often establish norms of appropriate usage and can act as moderators by sending warnings to members or even by deleting content and removing people from groups.[6] Josep, another of our interviewees in Barcelona, gives an example of this:

> **Josep:** I have a group called 'Camino de Santiago' and it is only about El Camino because any other commentary is forbidden.
> **Ariadna:** Who determined this norm?
> **Josep:** Me, I'm the admin and when I created the group, I specifically said that it was a space to talk about El Camino and that I didn't want messages like 'Merry Christmas' and birthday wishes.

Ariadna: And how did the members react to this norm?
Josep: In general, pretty well, but every now and then someone slips ... And then I either ignore them or if I see a pattern, I open an individual chat with them to let them know that it would be better to keep the conversation on topic. I'm a bit strict, I suppose.

Josep, Barcelona, 2019

The ability of admins to moderate content and manage participants became specifically relevant with the information overload that emerged from a combination of big groups and users' ability to easily share multimodal media on WhatsApp. Some of the admins' special powers, though, were not well received by users. In particular, the admin's ability to add people to a group without users consenting to it has been a site of contestation. Prior to 2019, admins could add anyone into a group as long as they had their phone number. In India, for example, a survey with WhatsApp users in 2017 found that one-sixth of WhatsApp users had been added to a group started by a political leader or party without their consent (Bansal & Garimella, 2019). Journalists published articles about how to get out of groups, such as jokingly recommending users to be as spammy as possible as a strategy to be kicked out by admins.[7]

As a response to users' complaints, WhatsApp has changed the Group feature over the years to better protect users. Between 2018 and 2019, WhatsApp changed its default settings to prevent admins repeatedly adding people to groups even after they had left.[8] The new settings also gave users different options regarding who could add them to groups: 'Everyone' (anyone with your phone number can add you to a group), 'My Contacts', (only people you have in your address book can add you to groups), or 'My Contacts Except'.[9] Relatedly, perhaps one of the most awaited design changes to groups was the ability to leave them quietly. As of August 2022, people can exit groups without leaving a trace that other group members can see. This allows users to exit large groups without being noticed, and it also eases the tension involved in deciding how to leave a group, as we unpack in chapter 3.

In November 2022, WhatsApp responded to user requests for larger sized groups by introducing the Communities feature, which allows for groups comprising up to 1,024 members. While it is too soon to evaluate users' uptake of and reactions to Communities, it is clear from WhatsApp's blogpost[10] that the change caters to the needs of organizations,[11] rather than to the needs of ordinary people wanting to communicate 'privately':

> we're aiming to raise the bar for how organizations communicate with a level of privacy and security not found anywhere else. The alternatives available today require trusting apps or software companies with a copy of their messages – and we think they deserve the higher level of security provided by end-to-end encryption.[12]

The introduction of document sharing feature in 2016 was already a game-changer in relation to workplace functionality, supplementing the ability to share photos, videos and voice messages in a scrolling, synchronous conversation, and making WhatsApp a versatile utility for workplace communications, replacing email, fax and scanner with an all-in-one platform. With Communities, organizations can bring together up to fifty different WhatsApp groups. Importantly, when creating a Community, users need to first create an announcement group that acts like a broadcasting tool to alert users of important messages. Many WhatsApp users strongly resisted the Communities feature. Soon after it was launched, users took to Twitter to issue pleas for organizations to stop adding people to Communities without their consent. Critics also warned that the feature could become an even greater superspreader of misleading and harmful information, a problem that had already haunted Meta with the expansion of Group size limits, making it a common site for rumour, gossip and the spread of other harmful content (Reuters, 2022).

WhatsApp groups afford intimacy and privacy. Indeed, WhatsApp has become closely associated with the qualities of intimate connections and strong social ties. Most of the groups that exist on the platform are family and friendship groups, local community and neighbourhood groups. However, in countries like Brazil, Malaysia and India these numbers are larger and groups act as public and semi-public forums (Banaji et al., 2019; Caetano et al., 2018), where context collapse may still occur. The implications of this reconfiguring of online socialities matter in our conceptualization of WhatsApp as a platform, as will be explored further in chapters 3 and 4.

Encryption

Encryption has been a key selling point for WhatsApp under Meta's stewardship. Technically, it means that the platform and third parties cannot access the content that individuals share. Symbolically, encryption allows WhatsApp to present itself as a privacy-friendly service while obscuring its role as a platform that uses people's data to monetize (Santos & Faure, 2018). But WhatsApp was not designed with this purpose in mind. Rather, Koum and Acton's aim was to develop a 'simple, personal, real time messaging'[13] app in which user data would not be the commodity:

> Remember, when advertising is involved you the user are the product. At WhatsApp, our engineers spend all their time fixing bugs, adding new features and ironing out all the little intricacies in our task of bringing rich, affordable, reliable messaging to every phone in the world. That's our product and that's our passion. Your data isn't even in the picture. We are simply not interested in any of it.[14]

Following this vision of protecting users' privacy, it is no surprise that WhatsApp founders saw end-to-end encryption as a logical technical evolution for its service. In November 2014, WhatsApp surprised its Android users with end-to-end encryption, enabled by default, but only for one-to-one text messages (images and videos were not encrypted, and group communication was not either). The rollout of this feature happened just nine months after WhatsApp announced its partnership with Meta,[15] and it helped Koum and Acton to reiterate their position that Meta's acquisition would not change their values. 'Respect' for users' privacy was 'coded' into their 'DNA', they claimed in a blogpost.[16] Acton had been working for months with software development group Open Whisper Systems to deploy the same encryption protocol that other platforms, such as Signal, were already using. However, WhatsApp was by far the largest platform to adopt this protocol, bringing encrypted communication to millions of ordinary users around the world.[17]

It was not until two years later, in April 2016, that WhatsApp announced, with a great deal of fanfare, the final rollout of end-to-end encryption by default for all WhatsApp users and for calls, messages, photos, videos, files and voice messages, including group chats.[18] The company published a blogpost about it, and users received pop-up messages that informed them that communication on the app was now encrypted. Not all information on WhatsApp is encrypted, though. Profile photos, user status messages and group information such as name, photo and description of groups[19] have never been encrypted, and the platform uses this information to moderate content on the platform. For example, WhatsApp uses algorithms to detect unlawful content such as child sexual abuse imagery in unencrypted information such as group profile pictures.[20]

The introduction of encryption was important for WhatsApp's founders, as it offered value for some of its most active user cohorts, such as activists and whistle-blowers, for whom the privacy afforded by end-to-end encryption is an important reason for using the service, as we explain in chapter 4. It is uncertain, though, that encryption is equally important for other everyday users on WhatsApp. For example, most of the users we interviewed in Barcelona did not know that WhatsApp was encrypted, and when encryption was explained to them, they were unimpressed by its alleged privacy affordances:

> **Ariadna:** Did you know that communication on WhatsApp is end-to-end encrypted?
> **Luis:** Not really.
> **Arianda:** It is, which means that WhatsApp cannot access nor read your messages. Do you care about this?
> **Luis:** I don't really care. I am always careful with what I send over WhatsApp and I am not part of any group in which we share confidential information ... The reality is that I am not much worried about information being encrypted or not.
>
> Luis, Barcelona, 2019

This finding aligns with previous literature that has found that WhatsApp users do not always understand the implications of end-to-end encryption and that, even when they do, they do not think encryption will protect their data from being misused by third parties (Dechand et al., 2019). In fact, this is precisely what happened with WhatsApp. A few months after rolling out encryption, in 2016, WhatsApp notified its users of an update of its Terms of Service and privacy policy.[21] The announcement informed them that WhatsApp was sharing user data with Meta, and by default, with other third-party companies. This data included users' phone numbers, usage and log activity (e.g., last time users used the service), as well as device information. This information was being used to improve people's experiences within Meta's services 'such as making product suggestions (for example, of friends or connections, or of interesting content) and showing relevant offers and ads on Facebook.[22] In a way, some of the users we interviewed in Barcelona intuitively knew about the limitations of encryption to protect their privacy and saw their

WhatsApp use as part of their broader social media and online interactions. Jordi told us:

> At a certain point I stopped worrying about my privacy. I have the feeling that we are always surveilled ... We're all on someone's file. It is what it is, nothing I can do about it ... Well, if I was a politician perhaps I would worry, and I would have three burner phones, and in a public space I would remove the battery of my phones. But this is not my case, so I do not worry about it.
>
> Jordi, 2019

But unlike Jordi, other WhatsApp users did worry about WhatsApp sharing data with Meta, and some of the app's most loyal user base, including activists, perceived this move as a breach of trust and voiced their plans to migrate to other services they perceived as being safer, such as Telegram (Tynan, 2016). Regulatory bodies also cared about WhatsApp sharing data with Meta. When Meta bought WhatsApp in 2014, it informed the European Commission that it would be unable to establish reliable automated matching between Facebook users' accounts and WhatsApp users' accounts. However, when WhatsApp announced updates to its Terms of Service and privacy policy in 2016, it was revealed that sharing user data among the companies was a possibility all along (see chapter 1 for context). This prompted the European Commission (EC) to fine[23] Facebook €110 million in 2017 for providing 'misleading information' about the privacy implications of WhatsApp's acquisition, such as the possibility of linking WhatsApp users' phone numbers with Facebook users' identities.

These contradictions over privacy issues grew as WhatsApp shifted to connect users to businesses and organizations with the launch of the WhatsApp Business App and the Business API in 2018. This prompted Koum and Acton to leave the company in dramatic circumstances, in 2018, allegedly over disagreement regarding the weakening of encryption as a result of Meta's plan to monetize WhatsApp and transform it into a business platform (as discussed in chapter 1). Finding himself under pressure for the handling of user data in all of his companies, Mark Zuckerberg responded to these criticisms with the announcement of more encryption as a roadmap to guarantee user 'privacy'. In a 2019 Facebook post, he wrote that the future of communication would 'increasingly shift to private, encrypted services where people can be confident what they say to each other stays secure and their messages and content won't stick around forever.'[24] In his 'privacy-focused' vision for social media, Zuckerberg mentioned WhatsApp as the example to follow:

> We plan to build this the way we've developed WhatsApp: focus on the most fundamental and private use case – messaging – make it as secure as possible, and then build more ways for people to interact on top of that, including calls, video chats, groups, stories, businesses, payments, commerce, and ultimately a platform for many other kinds of private services.
> Facebook post, 6 March 2019

The promise of encryption as a strategy to keep users safe was increasingly questionable not only because WhatsApp was sharing user data with Meta and third-party organizations, including law enforcement (Elkind et al., 2021), but also because of privacy loopholes within WhatsApp encryption itself. One of the most criticized privacy loopholes of WhatsApp's end-to-end-encryption was that chat backups to services like iCloud were not encrypted, as Russian entrepreneur and Telegram founder Pavel Durov highlighted in a 2019 BlogSpot titled 'Why WhatsApp will never be secure'. This loophole meant that information on WhatsApp could be easily 'accessed by hackers and law enforcement'.[25] User backlash over privacy issues linked to end-to-end encryption has pushed WhatsApp repeatedly to improve this feature, as demonstrated by the company's white paper on encryption, which has been updated six times since it was first published in 2016.[26] For example, WhatsApp implemented encryption to chat backups in 2021, two years after the issue was identified as an important design fault that was compromising user privacy.

WhatsApp has also responded to concerns over safety by implementing other user privacy controls over the years. For example, since 2022, users can decide who can view non-encrypted information such as their profile picture by choosing whether only contacts, everyone or nobody can see it (Malik, 2022). The platform has also launched various ways to communicate through ephemeral media to enhance 'private' communication. There are statuses[27] (like Instagram's and Facebook's stories) that allow users to share text, photo, video and GIF updates which disappear after 24 hours. Users can also set messages on chats to disappear after 24 hours, 7 days or 90 days; and they can also choose to send 'view once' messages. These design changes did not satisfy users, however, with complaints that people could take screenshots from 'view once' messages, making the feature less safe. In response, WhatsApp announced screenshot blocking for these 'view once' messages in 2022.

Despite all these design tweaks to give users more controls over their privacy, a new update in WhatsApp's privacy policy in 2021 proved how the platform's business model works against user privacy. It stated that WhatsApp collects and shares[28] information with Meta about user interactions with businesses via WhatsApp's Business App, including: transaction data (e.g., Facebook Pay or Shops in WhatsApp) and information on how users interact with businesses when using Meta services. Further, despite communication between people and businesses being end-to-end encrypted, encryption is weakened not only by the sharing of data between WhatsApp and Meta, but also because businesses can store WhatsApp chats within other Meta services[29] that are not encrypted, making this information available for advertisers (O'Flaherty, 2021). The new policy update received massive user backlash and some people flocked to other encrypted platforms such as Signal and Telegram. The update also incurred another fine, of €225 million, for Meta, this time by the Irish authorities,[30] who accused the company of failing to provide comprehensive information about how it was handling user data between WhatsApp and other Meta companies.

There are many tensions that arise from WhatsApp's competing design choices. On the one hand, WhatsApp sells its service as a way of communicating 'privately'. On the other hand, we have shown how the platform's end-to-end encryption is rather performative if WhatsApp has other ways to access user data and turn it into a commodity. Adding to the contradiction is the fact that the platform is technically evolving into a service that responds to the needs of organizations and companies, more so than ordinary users. This makes WhatsApp more of a 'public' forum for the sharing of information, professional communication and commercial exchange rather than an app to communicate privately. We explain this technical evolution in the next two sections.

Shareability and broadcast features

In the Introduction and chapter 1, we highlighted how WhatsApp has become a key platform for distributing, receiving and sharing news, with media sharing being associated with problematic uses of the platform, such as sharing health misinformation in the context of the COVID-19 pandemic. These user practices are often discussed in the scholarship without reference to the specific technical features that have enabled and constrained these practices, turning WhatsApp into a key tool for the dissemination of news and misinformation (Newman et al., 2018). In this chapter, these technical features – media-sharing plug-ins that allow the sharing of content from the open web and other platforms into WhatsApp, the Forward function, and Broadcast lists – are the main 'characters' that tell the story of how WhatsApp facilitates the spread of information and mediates public and private discussion.

In his book *The Age of Sharing*, Nicholas John (2017) examines 'sharing' as a key concept that defines contemporary practices in digital platforms and that conveys different meanings: sharing as intimacy, as communication and as an important practice that generates revenue for social media companies. On WhatsApp, the different meanings of sharing are apparent. WhatsApp promotes sharing (including the act of forwarding media) as part of communicating privately on the app: 'Share moments that matter'.[31] But, similar to other platforms, WhatsApp has other interests in people sharing. The platform has access to media forwarding patterns, and it uses this information as user metadata it shares with its parent company Meta.

Sharing plug-ins, the Forward function and Broadcast lists

The 'share' button plug-in, introduced in 2013, was a game-changer for media publishers wanting to tap into WhatsApp's growing user base. The plug-in allows content producers and media organizations to add a WhatsApp share button on their public interfaces so people can easily share their content to WhatsApp chats and groups via a simple click. This transformed WhatsApp into a site for the sharing of news and other media (Gil de Zúñiga et al., 2021; Newman et al., 2019), which we explain at length in chapter 4. But there are differences in the uptake of this feature by media organizations in different countries and regions around the world. For example, media outlets in countries where WhatsApp has a large user base, such as in Spain,[32] quickly introduced the WhatsApp 'share' button plug-in into their websites, while news outlets targeting audiences where WhatsApp is not that popular, like in Australia, did not.[33] The same strategy can be observed with other platforms that are making the sharing of their content on WhatsApp much easier. In 2022, Twitter announced it was testing the addition of a WhatsApp button under tweets, but only in India, one of WhatsApp's largest markets (Mehta, 2022).

The fact that sharing content from the open web and from other platforms to WhatsApp is almost frictionless, combined with the easy sharing of content within WhatsApp itself via its Forward function, have turned WhatApp into a medium where information spreads fast. This has forced WhatsApp to face similar problems to other more public-facing platforms, such as the spread of harmful content, including misinformation and hate speech. The fact that WhatsApp has had to find solutions to the spread of harmful content has also transformed WhatsApp into more than a chat app in the sense that it has had to invest resources into content moderation, a defining element of platforms (Gillespie, 2018; Gillespie et al., 2020).

WhatsApp was not originally designed as a tool to share media, though. In its early days, it was people's statuses – the sentences users wrote next to their names as answers to the question 'What's up' – that were the central driver of user engagement (Maíz-Arévalo, 2021; Olson, 2018). Prompts to encourage users to share what they were doing was a popular design choice at that time, also found in other apps, such as Twitter's 2016 tagline 'What are you doing?' (Burgess & Baym, 2020). As WhatsApp grew in popularity, and especially since the introduction of the Group chat in 2011, sharing media with friends, family and acquaintances became the new driver of user engagement and the platform's *stickiness* – and hence the Forward function gained centrality to the WhatsApp experience.

People on WhatsApp have different relationships with the Forward feature. The material from our interviews shows that users share news, memes and personal pictures for a range of different reasons – from maintaining interpersonal connections with others to sharing political information and facilitating activism. Jordi, one of our interviewees, explained this:

> I forward some jokes that I think can make some of my friends laugh. Sometimes I share a news article I know a specific person might be interested in. I have friends that send me news links from diverse news outlets, and when I see a news article from an outlet I like I send that link to friends who I know don't read these news, but could be interested in the topic covered by the journalist. I have also sent some political information, when there are demonstrations and we have to get organised with friends to meet up to be present there.
>
> Jordi, Barcelona, 2019

Bakare et al. (2022) and Herrero-Diz et al. (2020) also found that, like Jordi, WhatsApp users tend to forward messages that they think will have a special value to the recipients. One downside of this tendency has been noted in Brazil, where surveys have found that people who are more engaged in discussing politics on WhatsApp are significantly more likely to share misinformation on the platform (Rossini et al., 2021). One of our interviewees in Barcelona, Andreu, admitted to forwarding messages close to his heart, especially those related to Catalan politics, without paying attention to whether the content was accurate:

> **Andreu:** I am a Catalan Independentist, and I discuss this topic in several of my WhatsApp groups. When I receive information about our Independence process, I always forward it.
> **Ariadna:** Do you confirm that the information you share is legit?
> **Andreu:** I think I often make the mistake of too easily believing everything about this topic [laughs]. I say 'I make the mistake' because I know I should verify some of the information I receive before sending it, but I usually don't.
>
> Andreu, Barcelona, 2019

With the Forward function becoming a core driver of user engagement on WhatsApp, 'democratically dysfunctional' content sharing, a practice whereby users spread misinformation in their own trusted networks (Chadwick et al., 2018), has become commonplace. Numerous actors, including public and political figures, have taken advantage of this, using WhatsApp as a medium to quickly spread falsehoods and misleading and harmful content. This trend is further examined in relation to the concept of 'information disorder' in chapter 4. In countries like India and Brazil, the problem of misinformation spreading via WhatsApp has been linked to nefarious material consequences, including mob violence. In these countries, groups tend to be larger than average, communication through public groups is popular and political parties have embraced the platform to mobilize their supporters and manipulate campaigns. In India, for example, the local press was already reporting in 2014 that the easy forwarding of rumours via WhatsApp was triggering the lynching of innocent people in the country, another example we will return to in chapter 4 (TNN, 2014). It was not until 2018, though, that WhatsApp started reacting to this problem, largely because of the international coverage of Indian mob violence which began with rumours shared on WhatsApp groups (BBC, 2018; Rajput et al., 2018).

Since 2018, the platform has announced various measures to curb the spread of harmful content and conduct.[34] It rolled out labels on Forwarded messages so that users could differentiate between messages that had been forwarded from friends and family, and external content. If a family member sent a WhatsApp chain message to their WhatsApp family group, a 'forwarded' label would appear at the top of the message, to indicate that the message had not been originally written or created by the sender. Importantly, WhatsApp also applied limits on the number of times content could be forwarded to recipients. But while in India content could only be forwarded to five recipients at a time, in other countries the forward limit was set to twenty recipients. In Brazil, advocacy groups pleaded with WhatsApp to lower its forwarding limit from twenty recipients to five (as was the case in India) to curb the spread of hoaxes and harmful propaganda during the country's 2018 general election. But WhatsApp dismissed this call for help, and, in October, far-right candidate Jair Bolsonaro won the election, with observers attributing his victory, to some degree, to his use of WhatsApp to mobilize supporters (Chagas, 2022). As WhatsApp found itself increasingly featured at the centre of controversies regarding the spread of harmful content at a global scale (Newman et al., 2018), in 2019 the company finally reduced forwarding limits to five chats globally.[35] The same year, WhatsApp labelled 'viral' messages with double arrows and the sentence 'forwarded many times' to indicate that this content did not originate from a close contact.

By the time that it was clear that WhatsApp was a key platform for the spread of harmful content in many parts of the world, the platform published a white paper (WhatsApp, 2019) to inform the public about how it was pursuing content moderation, in spite of encryption. In it, WhatsApp claimed that it was using machine learning to proactively detect 'abusive behaviour' such as spam and ban suspicious accounts 'at registration, during messaging, and in response to user reports'. The numbers provided by WhatsApp demonstrated that the platform was indeed being used as a tool for abuse: over 2 million accounts per month were removed for bulk or automated behaviour, a pattern that was common during elections where certain actors attempted to send messages at scale. This is a practice that chapter 4 examines in more detail in relation to elections in India, Brazil and Indonesia. WhatsApp also noted that it was scanning unencrypted information like profile photos for child exploitative imagery, and that it had modified the way the core chatting app was designed, based on how it was being used.

The 2019 white paper, in laying out how WhatsApp was fighting abuse, stated that the platform 'is not a broadcast platform' (p. 4). And yet, the platform has, over the years, developed the very features that serve the purpose of broadcast messaging, including messaging from one-to-many and from many-to-many. The Broadcast list, introduced in late 2013, is an example of such a feature, as is the Group feature, and also Communities. All these features allow large numbers of users, unknown to one another, to receive messages from a single source. As chapter 4 explores in greater detail, journalists and politicians use Broadcast lists to circulate messages to large numbers of people in their contact lists, effectively enlisting those contacts into a 'public' through a broadcast address.

All in all, WhatsApp's content moderation efforts such as adding friction to forwards or its use of machine learning to detect abusive conduct are at odds with design choices that promote the use of WhatsApp as a broadcasting tool and as a 'public' discussion forum and space for the sharing of media. It does not matter that there are limits to forwards if users can reach thousands of people at once via Broadcast list, Groups and Communities (Dixit, 2022). In addition, WhatsApp is interested in people sharing content because the platform has the ability to turn sharing patterns into useful information for other stakeholders, such as advertisers. Further, other WhatsApp features such as the WhatsApp Business App and the Business API are also in contradiction with the platform's public statements about user safety and privacy.

Business-oriented features

The launch of the WhatsApp Business App and the Business API in 2018 marked a key moment in WhatsApp's transformation into a tool for businesses, which is central to our argument conceptualizing WhatsApp as a platform. It also signalled a new path for monetizing WhatsApp. Through the rollout of business-oriented solutions, Meta was, for the first time, making money directly from WhatsApp by charging companies a fee to use these services and selling them 'click to messaging' ads via the Facebook platform, which we examine in more detail in chapter 5. WhatsApp's uniqueness as a platform for commercial activity can be found in the way it builds upon informal cultures of small business exchange that grew 'organically' in key markets where WhatsApp was the preferred platform for everyday communication. In Brazil, for example, people have been buying and selling products informally on WhatsApp since 2011 (Marasciulo, 2022), and in Kenya businesses have also incorporated WhatsApp as part of their communication with customers since its early beginnings (Mbote, 2014). In fact, when thinking about the biography of WhatsApp, it is important to acknowledge how the features tailored for businesses emerged from user practices: commercial operators were using WhatsApp as a tool for business long before this use was formalized and monetized via changes in WhatApp's design. Our interviews in Barcelona also bear witness to this fact. Jaume, for example, told us that when he was working for a hearing care international retailer, some of the company's intermediaries used to text him over WhatsApp to pressure him to quickly answer quotes they had sent him.

As of February 2022, WhatsApp's website menu (whatsapp.com) shows various options that are an indication of where the platform is heading (figure 2.1). Under the Features tab, WhatsApp displays what the platform has on offer: message privately, stay connected, build community, express yourself and WhatsApp Business. WhatsApp Business is the only option that, when clicked on, redirects people to a completely new website[36] (business.whatsapp.com) with its own menu showing different navigation paths: products, resources, blog, developers, partners. Unlike WhatsApp's main website, Meta's logo is visible in the landing page of WhatsApp's business solutions, which creates the visual effect of an umbrella domain hosting a specific product – a pretty accurate representation of the reality that WhatsApp is a key piece within Meta's industrial development and growth (Novet, 2022). Since 2018, WhatsApp has launched two main technical features aimed at connecting users with small and large businesses: the WhatsApp Business App and the Business API. While email and call centres have been key tools for companies to connect with and make economic transactions with clients, WhatsApp sees 'live chat' as the new way to sell products, communicate with and support customers.[37]

By studying these features, we show how WhatsApp's evolution into a platform for businesses creates issues around data protection and privacy. The development of WhatsApp business products not only allows users' private data to be accessed by businesses, but, by allowing advertising messages to target users' private WhatsApp accounts, it also alters how people have hitherto experienced the platform, as simple, reliable and ad-free.

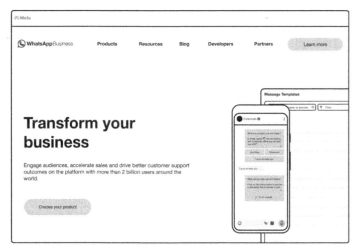

Figure 2.1: Artist's impression of the landing page of WhatsApp's business solution. Art provided by Phoebe Tan.

The WhatsApp Business App

In September 2017, WhatsApp announced it was developing tools to help small businesses and large companies to use chat more effectively to communicate with customers. A few months later, in January 2018, the WhatsApp Business App for Android phones was launched in Indonesia, Italy, Mexico, the UK and the US.[38] In a blogpost, WhatsApp announced the introduction of this free business-oriented app, declaring it was designed in response to user demands, especially in key markets such as India and Brazil:

> People all around the world use WhatsApp to connect with small businesses they care about – from online clothing companies in India to auto parts stores in Brazil ... Over 80% of small businesses in India and Brazil say WhatsApp helps them both communicate with customers and grow their business today (Source: Morning Consult study).[39]

The app includes features not present in the core mobile chat app, such as automated away messages, shortcuts and a business profile feature that verifies a WhatsApp Business App user as a bona fide business. In 2019, the Business App was launched on IOS and expanded to Brazil and Germany, and new redesigns were introduced, such as the catalogue feature that enables businesses to showcase products for sale. In just one year after the launch of the WhatsApp Business App, the platform reported that 5 million businesses were using the service.[40]

The WhatsApp Business App is tailored to facilitate communications between small business owners and their customers, display products and facilitate shipping. It can be seen as akin to both a customer relations management (CRM) tool and a storefront, where goods are exhibited through the catalogues function, and traded through the carts function. In some markets, such as India, products can be paid for in the storefront using WhatsApp Pay, a system that enables the instant transfer of funds between two accounts of participating banks, via WhatsApp, which we cover in more detail in chapter 5. The Business App is free to use, although WhatsApp has repeatedly said that in the future they intend to monetize this product by either charging businesses a fee for using the app, or by charging a fee for a premium[41] version (Constine, 2017).

While businesses have to download the Business App to chat and sell products to people, customers communicate with businesses via the main mobile chat app. That is, for everyday users, interacting with business occurs within the boundaries of the same app interface they use to communicate with family, friends and acquaintances. Everyday users can recognize business accounts on the main chat app because these are labelled as such. There are three main ways customers can identify business accounts. The default business account option only displays the phone number of the account holder above the words 'Business Account'. If the business has been authenticated by WhatsApp as a bona fide business, the name of the business, instead of the phone number, will appear regardless of whether the customer has saved the business to their contact list. A third category is verified businesses, which have a green badge[42] against their name after they have gone through an authentication process[43] with WhatsApp. Businesses answer customer requests on the mobile phones where the Business App is installed, and only four devices can be added to the same account name. To overcome the limitations of the Business App and to cater for the needs of bigger businesses, WhatsApp also offers the WhatsApp Business API as a more sophisticated product for reaching out to large customer bases.

WhatsApp Business API

WhatsApp launched its Business API in August 2018, which the company refers to as its Business *Platform* (emphasis added). WhatsApp uses the term platform here in its computational meaning: 'a programmable infrastructure upon which other software can be built and run, like ... information services that provide APIs so developers can design additional layers of functionality' (Gillespie, 2017). The Business API has no front-end interface (it is not a stand-alone app like the Business App) but allows medium to large companies to connect with WhatsApp users via WhatsApp business solution providers. These 'providers' are professional customer messaging and workspace organizing software companies that WhatsApp recognizes as legitimate software firms and with whom large companies can partner to connect with customers via WhatsApp. In a sense, the Business API, which is hosted on Meta's data infrastructure via the Meta for Developers platform, can be considered as a 'bridge' or a 'point of contact' between large businesses, such as airlines and hospitality companies, and regular WhatsApp users, via professional software companies.

Unlike the Business App, which is free, medium and large companies pay a fee to use the Business API. In fact, when WhatsApp launched the Business API, the press covered the launch as the first time WhatsApp was making money directly from the services it offered (Constine, 2018). When medium and large companies message customers through the WhatsApp Business API, they are charged per conversation, which includes all messages delivered within a 24-hour period. Companies are only charged when they exceed 1,000 messages per month, and if they use a business solution provider, they need to connect with them directly to coordinate the payment via a credit line offered by WhatsApp (Business Help Centre, n.d.). In 2022, WhatsApp introduced the WhatsApp Cloud API – a cloud-based version of the Business API that is hosted on Meta's infrastructure and which was designed to eliminate server expenses for small companies (Perez, 2022).

The problem with WhatsApp's business products (both the Business App and the Business API) is that they compromise user privacy. While chats between customers and a business remain encrypted, like regular peer-to-peer chats, they are not strictly private, as some businesses employ third-party non-encrypted cloud services to manage and store their chats.[44] WhatsApp shows users when businesses are using third-party software companies to manage chats in an attempt to be transparent. But the fact that WhatsApp chats are managed by third parties and stored outside WhatsApp creates a privacy loophole. Further, the technological evolution of WhatsApp business solutions in key markets indicates that Meta wants users to do more than chat on WhatsApp. In Brazil, WhatsApp tested an in-app business directory feature called Business Search that allows users to find businesses from within the app instead of having to search for them on Google (Singh, 2022b). This means that for ordinary users, the WhatsApp core mobile chat app is evolving into something like a superapp, where users will be able to do multiple things from one central interface. But, in a technical sense, WhatsApp as a platform is more than that – WhatsApp is building a technical infrastructure that goes beyond one interface to include, increasingly and in particular, multiple apps, software, features, services and APIs designed and developed exclusively for businesses.

The development of these business products has been possible thanks to WhatsApp's 2016 and 2021 Terms of Service updates. The first update allowed WhatsApp to share user data with Meta, and the 2021 update allowed Meta's cloud service to act as an intermediary between businesses and users' messaging communication. WhatsApp's technical evolution into a tool for businesses has led WhatsApp to develop new Terms of Service *just* for businesses, as well as other policies targeted specifically at this type of stakeholder.[45] This means that WhatsApp's platformization in a technical sense is increasingly driven to satisfy business users, which we argue is having deep implications for everyday users' experience on WhatsApp, contributing to its evolution away from Acton and Koum's vision and philosophy. We further develop this point in chapter 5.

Conclusion

In this chapter we have provided a detailed account of WhatsApp's technical dimensions. We have explained, through a short review of its main technical features, how WhatsApp's design has evolved hand in hand with its end-users, including ordinary users, media organizations and businesses. To understand WhatsApp's evolution into a global communication and business platform, one must look at how this technology is used in key markets such as Africa, Europe, South Asia and Latin America. Perhaps WhatsApp came to the attention of millions of Americans and other users after Meta bought it in 2014. By then, though, the platform was already incredibly popular in other parts of the world.[46] That year, Indian media outlets were reporting how WhatsApp was widely used by businesses and how people had 'WhatsAppitis' (Sonwalkar, 2014). Spain was one of the leaders in the use of WhatsApp as early as in 2012[47] (Reventós, 2012), and Brazilians had been using the platform to buy and sell products since 2011 (Marasciulo, 2022). In other words, WhatsApp is evolving not because of how it is used in the United States or in Australia but owing to how people use it and negotiate with it in many other parts of the world, most notably in the Global South.

We have also explained that there are many contradictions arising from WhatsApp's design. The platform insists that its products facilitate private communication and it sells end-to-end encryption as a guarantee of this promise (Santos & Faure, 2018). But user privacy is hard to maintain within WhatsApp's current technological development. First, the progressive increase in group size – with Communities being the last iteration in this direction – and the business-oriented features are transforming WhatsApp's main mobile app into a space where communication among strangers is increasingly the norm. WhatsApp is building interoperability to help organizations and businesses to chat with people at scale. This means that these stakeholders can chat with people beyond the main mobile app – for instance, through third-party software developer companies or through WhatsApp's other web and app 'instances' (Nieborg & Helmond, 2019) such as the Desktop and Business apps. Interoperability also means that these stakeholders can easily store WhatsApp communications in other services that are often unencrypted, which compromises user privacy. Second, WhatsApp has been sharing user data with Meta since at least 2016, when the platform updated its Terms of Service announcing this change. This was perceived as a breach of trust by some WhatsApp users who had started using the service prior to Meta's acquisition because they believed that the company was not interested in user data. Since then, it has become clear that WhatsApp user data has become a key commodity for Meta – it is used as valuable information for businesses. And, for platforms that see people's data as a commodity, user privacy is never a priority (van Dijck & Poell, 2013).

3
Everyday Uses of WhatsApp

Each morning, like millions of people all over the world, we (Emma, Amelia and Ariadna) spend our initial waking moments immersed in WhatsApp, updating ourselves on the developments of the previous night. On a typical morning, we are likely to find a string of messages of different kinds, ranging from very public 'broadcast' type messages to strictly private one-on-ones, with targeted corporate messages, commercial transactions, and neighbourly, friendly and family chats sitting somewhere in between. A car insurance service notifies Emma that her policy is due for renewal, and one of Ariadna's family groups sends her a video of her nephew's first steps. Amelia creates a group for visiting co-researchers on a project, and her personal trainer sends her a workout update and tells her to share a photo to prove that she isn't slacking off.

In this chapter we develop an account of some of these everyday uses of WhatsApp. Drawing on concepts of 'everyday' and 'ordinary' life (Highmore, 2002) we draw attention to those practices that are so mundane, so ordinary and routinized that they often get taken-for-granted, such that they have 'fallen into the background' (Bucher, 2021, p. 96). We might describe this by referring to the ways technologies become familiar and unremarkable as they become incorporated into the habitual spaces, practices and flow of daily life. In this sense, they are often viewed in opposition to the realm of 'exceptional things and events, or formal, proper occurrences in the realm of public life' (Goggin, 2021, p. 119).

Our focus on the everyday in this chapter distinguishes 'ordinary' uses from professional, government or business uses. It is necessary to establish this distinction because, by nature, WhatsApp draws all manner of communications into the everyday, collapsing the distinctions between 'private' and 'public'. On WhatsApp, activities that could be considered elements of public life, like consuming the news, or the sharing of public service announcements, leak into the crevices of the quotidian; the 'always on, always available' nature of the platform (Matassi et al., 2019, p. 2183) has the effect of condensing genres of communication that were once separate, leading to the 'everydayizing' of everything. For example, on WhatsApp, business transactions may involve use of everyday linguistic devices such as emojis (Lim, 2015), and political campaigning can rely on uses of memes (Baulch et al., 2022).

This chapter is not concerned with the 'everdayizing' of everything on WhatsApp, but rather is focused on specific kinds of everyday non-professional use by ordinary users. We contend that it is important to understand the qualities of everyday practices to appreciate the story of WhatsApp's widespread uptake. In the Introduction, we discussed network effects, which correlates the value of a platform to the size of its network. Network effects is one of the concepts that is useful to understanding WhatsApp's success, but it glosses over the rich cultures of use that evolve as the network spreads. Gillespie (2018) draws attention to how users 'swarm' platforms, repurposing technical features to their own communicative needs, and we argue that such 'swarming' is as important to WhatsApp's value as the size of its network. As Burgess and Baym (2020) argue, the success or failure of platforms rests on their amenability to user appropriation. Such appropriation is an important part of WhatsApp's evolution – not only as it relates to the growth of its user base, but also to its embeddedness in users' everyday lives.

The term 'platform vernacular' (Gibbs et al., 2015) aptly describes the everyday practices that result from user appropriation of WhatsApp. A vernacular is a distinct form of a language that is spoken in a distinct region. It is a term that acknowledges the various possible ways of speaking any one language. For example, the way people speak French in the north of France is different to the way they speak it in the south. There is a northern vernacular and a southern one. Similarly, a 'combination of styles, grammars and logics' marks communication on different platforms as distinct, such that we can speak of *platform* vernaculars: 'shared (but not static) conventions and grammars of communication, which emerge from the ongoing interactions between platforms and users' (Gibbs et al., 2015, p. 257).

Below, we organize our discussion of WhatsApp's platform vernacular into three categories of practice: connection/disconnection, expression and public display. In the first category, we include practices that emerge from people's use of the platform to connect with family and friends. These practices highlight the nature of WhatsApp's 'stickiness' (Chen et al., 2018): how people rely on the platform to maintain their personal stake in social networks. In the second category, we include the ways users infiltrate the spaces of the platform with expressive content, such as stickers or memes (see, e.g., Matamoros-Fernández, 2020), and the ways they develop new communicative norms by using the platform. These practices demonstrate users' appropriative bent: they 'everydayize' WhatsApp chat by drawing it into everyday communicative norms, involving humour, emotion and etiquette. The third category involves the ways users exploit WhatsApp as an arena for public display, via statuses, 'online' and 'last seen' notification and profile images. These elements highlight similarities between WhatsApp and social media platforms; the term 'chat app' invokes peer-to-peer conversation that is strictly private, but there are clearly very public dimensions to the ways WhatsApp facilitates peer-to-peer engagement. Users can, for example, either actively or inadvertently, craft information about themselves that, by default, is made available to all users in their contact list. These users can encounter and observe such public-facing information about users in their contact list without directly engaging with the creator of the content in encrypted chat. In other words, WhatsApp provides users with a number of tools for publicly displaying themselves; its combination of private chat and public display enable the platform to function in a manner that resembles social media.

Connectedness and disconnection

Increasingly, people rely on WhatsApp to extend connections with family and close friends, or with partners or potential lovers. WhatsApp is a place where these relationships evolve and grow through conversation, sharing personal news, holiday or family snaps, or jokes and laughter. For many people, WhatsApp lies at the core of the networks of strong ties that anchor us; it is a necessary part of the way we care for meaningful relationships. In this section we draw on our personal experiences, interviews with users, and studies published by other scholars, to bring to light the ways users incorporate WhatsApp within the dynamics of friendship, family or relationships with intimate partners. This process of incorporation shows how users 'swarm' WhatsApp, but also highlights how, by virtue of its architecture, the platform affords new possibilities, and extends relationships in new directions. For example, as we will discuss below, users rely on WhatsApp not only to simply connect, but also to manage their strong tie connections by using WhatsApp features, including read receipts, last seen and notifications.

The WhatsApp Group feature is vital to the way many people use the platform to maintain their stake in social networks. Enduring, long-term groups, such as family groups, are a feature of many users' experience, but so are ephemeral or temporary groups tied to particular events. For example, people create groups to organize birthday parties, to go on a trip or meet up for dinner. In some cases, these groups may be abandoned after the activity ceases, but in others they may simply lie fallow until it is time to plan another activity with the same group.

In 2021 and again in 2022, Emma's research assistant, Gabriel Pereira, undertook interviews with WhatsApp users in Malaysia to learn more about the different kinds of WhatsApp groups with which they most often engage. In the interviews, Gabriel invited participants to draw maps of their WhatsApp group landscape and attribute qualities of their own choosing to the different groups. He used the maps to guide his interviews with the participants about what happened in each of the groups.

The mapping exercise and the interviews help us to understand the variety of ways people use the Groups function to invest in and care for the relationships that are meaningful to them. Some users categorized the groups in terms of importance, and in some of these maps, family WhatsApp groups were not present at all (Janice), in others they were a minor presence (Pritha), and for other users still their maps included whole complexes of family groups (Zebedee). For example, the name of Janice's primary group, 'Hol' the tea sis' designates the group as a private realm where gossip is exchanged. Janice explained that 'Hol' the tea' alludes to the expression 'spill the tea', 'which basically means to gossip or to share information ... juicy information ... so this is the group where we spill all the tea about things that are happening because the members of this group are all part of the Department of Psychology [at Monash Malaysia], myself included, so this is where we kind of spill all the gossip'. Others, such as Zebedee, mapped landscapes that included whole complexes of family groups, including designated groups for cousins, siblings, extended family and immediate family.

Family groups

Users on WhatsApp typically have one to multiple family groups (e.g., groups with core family members, with in-laws, with extended family, with siblings or cousins, and groups with family members plus partners). The WhatsApp users Ariadna interviewed in Barcelona expressed that one of the things they like most about WhatsApp is the sense of being connected to loved ones and having more regular communication with kin living close by, as well as overseas. They noted that while they were not always regular participants in other groups (e.g., friends groups, groups of work colleagues), they interacted in family groups, especially with core family members, even if it was just to react to others' messages. Our research shows that family groups mostly serve to keep each other 'up to date' and to coordinate meetups, but they can also be spaces to share jokes and information about news and events. Some interviewees in Barcelona noted how family WhatsApp groups can bring to the fore pre-existing family dynamics and differences in communication styles. For example, Jordi began to notice how his wife's close relationship with their daughters manifested in their exclusive 'girls' WhatsApp group. He tried, and failed, to recreate such a group with his sons, and this caused him to acknowledge the different qualities of father–son and mother–daughter relationships:

> **Jordi:** I have a WhatsApp group with my wife and our kids, but my wife has a separate group with our daughters and they meet up and go on trips together, and one day I said to myself: 'I want this too!' So, I created a group with my sons to travel with them too... But we haven't gone anywhere, the group doesn't work.
> **Ariadna:** (laughs) And did you try other strategies to reanimate the group?
> **Jordi:** Oh no. When I realized it didn't work, I said let's leave it, let's not try to reproduce a thing that works with the girls but not with us, really.
>
> Jordi, Barcelona, 2019

Our interviews with Malaysian participants showed how WhatsApp family groups can also introduce new dynamics: such groups can be used to draw out, perhaps even construct, alliances and affinities within immediate and extended families. Zebedee relayed how participants used admin powers to create a 'caucus' for dealing with the problems of a particular member, who was temporarily removed from the group, showing how the admin function affords power play and manoeuvring within family complexes.

> Let's say we need to speak in particular about someone, and how to manage them without the feeling like they're going to be attacked, we will tell them, the thing about family is that we're open: 'We're removing you out of the group so we can discuss how to best solve your problem', then they come back after that.
>
> Zebedee, Kuala Lumpur, 2021

Other users spoke of how group participants used features of the Group function to exert power, either by shaping the discourse in particular ways or including/excluding people from the group. For example, in explaining how her family group came to be named 'Global family v2', Pritha spoke of how her grandfather had used his powers as an admin of the group to protest the group dynamics, which he felt marginalized him.

> **Gabriel:** After Palmilla Gang Gang you have Global Family V2.
> **Pritha:** Right so this one is my family chat. This extends to our external relations as well, so like my granddad's sisters even. Even though they are based in India and Canada, some of us are based in Australia, the US as well. So, this is meant for like a central chat for everyone. Version 2 is because the version 1, my granddad got upset for some reason and felt he wasn't important, and just kicked everybody out of the group, and all of us were like, 'Dude what?' So now this is version 2, the revamped one.
>
> Pritha, Kuala Lumpur, 2021

Archetypical group behaviours

With the Group feature becoming part and parcel of the WhatsApp experience, archetypal user group behaviours have emerged. For example, *Time Out London*[1] reported on the 'top five worst people in your WhatsApp groups'. The list included 'the lurker' (those who do not participate in conversations); 'the debt collector' (people who only comment when they need something); the 'constant monologist' (those that cannot stop talking about their life); 'the spam bot' (people who always share viral content and memes); and 'the deserter' (that person who suddenly leaves a group).

Our interview data from Barcelona and Malaysia unearthed some of these archetypical behaviours, although interviewees did not always attribute negative qualities to them. Users interviewed by Ariadna and Amelia shared their experiences with, or identified as, people who frequently shared viral content, memes, and 'good morning' and 'good night' messages. While some, particularly younger, users found these messages irritating, many older users we interviewed expressed their joy at receiving and sending them. When Ariadna asked Ana about the subject matter of her WhatsApp group chat with her friends, she offered the following:

> **Ariadna:** What do you discuss in the group with your three close friends?
> **Ana:** They send me 'Good morning' and 'Good evening' messages every day.
> **Ariadna:** And you also respond 'Good morning' and 'Good evening'?
> **Ana:** Not always, but quite often, yes [she looks at her phone and scrolls the chat to show Ariadna one instance of this ritual]. See! There you are: Bon dia! Bona nit [Good morning, good night].
>
> Ana, Barcelona, 2019

In Malaysia, Amelia found that older users frequently shared memes containing inspirational quotes or religious

Figure 3.1: Artist's impression of "Good morning" messages and inspirational quotes which circulate in family WhatsApp groups. Art provided by Phoebe Tan.

messages giving thanks and blessings. Many older users shared such messages frequently throughout the day, sometimes one after another (see figure 3.1). Some of these memetic messages were so popular they were shared by multiple family members, appearing multiple times in the same discussion.

Strategies for managing groups and chats over time

Other interviewees identified a more malicious kind of spam bot, who routinely shared misinformation to WhatsApp groups. Different people had different ways of dealing with such users. Some, such as Jordi, chose to confront them, but only if such users were 'serial offenders'. Jordi alluded to the thought required when choosing when to respond to 'spam bot' users to question the veracity of forwarded information:

> **Ariadna:** How do you react with misleading information forwarded via your groups?
> **Jordi:** Sometimes I have intervened, but I don't do it often because you might be perceived as a smart-ass. Some people forward so many things that in the end one says: 'well, that's enough'. There's a tendency to forward everything ...
> **Ariadna:** And what do you do in these cases?
> **Jordi:** I have sometimes asked group members if they have verified the information they just forwarded and people usually respond well to these call outs if they haven't.
> Jordi, Barcelona, 2019

Jordi's testimony is validated by previous literature on sharing and contesting misinformation within Groups. Rossini et al. (2021, p. 2432) found that, on WhatsApp, people are more likely 'to experience, perform, and witness social correction' than on other platforms such as Facebook, which the authors attribute to 'closer social ties' being found on WhatsApp, that might afford 'a sense of safety that supports these behaviors'. Others have documented other processes of norm setting within groups to control forwarded media. For example, Sarkar (2022) explains how some group admins enforce a 'no-forwards-please' rule to delimit non-relevant information. Nonetheless, close social ties can also produce avoidant behaviours when it comes to correcting misinformation shared by group members (Chadwick et al., 2022). This has particularly been noted in cultural contexts where young people are 'deferential toward family members, especially the elderly' (p. 12), as found in Amelia's interviews with young people in Malaysia who referred to WhatsApp family groups as places where high volumes of misinformation often circulated, but where it was rarely corrected:

> I just don't open them anymore. I'm not sure how real or fake they are [news articles shared by her dad] so I just

ignore. Then I'm at the dinner table and he says 'look, look' and I have to read it. I'm not sure where he gets it from, but he has friends who share it and he shares here. Lots of the time I just roll my eyes. Sometimes I read and wish I didn't.

Verona, Kuala Lumpur, 2018

Emma's interviews in Malaysia revealed alternative strategies for managing 'spam bot' users in groups, but they involved use of platform tools and other methods to 'mute' notifications. This could involve disallowing various kinds of notifications for new messages (sounds, banners, voice announcements). This is one way of dealing with particularly 'noisy' groups. Another way is to simply archive groups or contacts. When relegated to a dedicated 'archived' folder, messages from those groups or contacts will not elicit notifications, even if the user has not disallowed notifications in their settings:

> Usually I don't bother reading the hundreds of messages. I would just, at the end of it, ask if there is anything I should take note of because sometimes that thread of messages may not be related to me. So, I would just ask. So that's one way to cope, and then if there are ongoing messages, which I think are not important, and there is no action for me to take, I would just mute it. Thank God for the mute function!
>
> Amanda, Kuala Lumpur, 2021

> This one group, I think it's a community group, there's about a hundred of us inside, so in a day, there's about a hundred messages. It's just too many, I would usually just mute the group.
>
> Chelsi, Kuala Lumpur, 2021

As well as turning off notifications or 'muting' as a way of managing 'noisy' groups, our participants also talked about disabling the 'last seen' and 'read receipts' functions in WhatsApp. Users told us that they chose to hide information about when they last opened WhatsApp, and whether they had read a message or not, so that they could respond at a later time to messages already read, without fear of offending interlocutors who may expect an immediate response. Some, such as Albreda, opted to turn off last seen but to enable 'read receipts', as this gave them recourse to 'leaving people on seen' (reading their message but delaying the reply) as a way of expressing displeasure with the person.

> The 'last seen', you know 'last seen at ...' whatever time that you were last on WhatsApp, I switched off that because, honestly, when you switch that on people want you to reply to them. Like, 'Oh my God you were online at this time, but you can't reply to my message?' ... I switched off my 'last seen' but the blue tick is on because if I ignore someone, I want that person to know that I'm ignoring them.
> Albreda, Kuala Lumpur, 2021

> I make [the read receipt and last seen] invisible actually because I think, at one point, it came to a point where people were expecting an instant reply .... So, I keep it invisible, just so that in a way people are being forced to respect my time.
> Amanda, Kuala Lumpur, 2021

> My blue ticks are hidden, and my 'last seen' is hidden as well .... Since the first day the blue tick was invented, I knew that we could turn it off.
> Chelsi, Kuala Lumpur, 2021

Expressive content

Texting

One of the effects of the global spread of mobile instant messaging is the rise of multimodal 'texting', including the exchange of links, text messages, photos, voice recordings and stickers, as a way of conducting private dialogue across space and time. This development cannot be attributed to WhatsApp specifically, but it informs how users attribute meaning to WhatsApp as a whole and its various features individually. As mentioned in the previous chapters, from its inception WhatsApp was positioned by its founders as an app whose unique selling point was its capacity to offer free text messaging and, later, free voice calls. Although corporate packaging does not differentiate the value of these two features, they have attained very distinct cultural meanings in the process of user adoption. For example, in some contexts, voice calls are often derided through association with older users, suggesting that it is an outdated mode of communication, preferred by those who are less knowledgeable about texting vernaculars. In Matassi et al. (2019), a 72-year-old woman reported that her daughter-in-law told her that, whenever the phone rings 'it's either you or my mom' (p. 2191). Implicit in these derisions is the idea that other types of uses – e.g., multimodal texting – are preferred. By positioning different features in a hierarchy, users construct patterns of preferred use. In response to her daughter-in-law's comment, the 72-year-old woman ceased calling, and began communicating exclusively via text.

The rise of free text messaging has prompted users to express themselves in new ways. For example, Baxter (2018) discusses the use of 'utterance chunking', which refers to the way users typically break up a message into chunks, rather than presenting it as a single, long block. This is a practice users would have avoided when using SMS, which in many contexts incurs a cost for each message sent. With WhatsApp, users can send as many messages as they like without incurring additional costs and this encourages 'chunking'. In the example provided by Baxter, chunking enables users of a WhatsApp cancer support group to 'convey diverse types of information, or to offer inviting leads, each of which might appeal to different members of the group' (2018, p. 374). It offers a strategy for users to secure the attention and participation of others in the group, which is key to the affective work that users perform, and which enhances the 'stickiness' of WhatsApp. In the excerpt below, one of the support group members, Ravi, employs utterance chunks to convey a set of complex information, including a number of 'inviting leads':

1. Ravi |16.19|Hey friends long time. I often wonder how we are doing.
2. Ravi |16.20|I've had 2 doses of iphosphamide and am coping OK. The 'inner Trump' is not growing and my belly is softer!
3. Ravi |16.20| And am doing lots with friends and decided to get a little dog!
4. Ravi |16.22|Has anyone looked into high dose vit C? My medics say be careful cause it could protect the cancer but this seems more theoretical. Views/networking/help most welcome.
5. Ravi |16.22|Big ☺ from me for Easter!

Baxter (2018, p. 373)

In the message above, Ravi uses utterance chunking to perform affective work, to manage the pace of its delivery and reception, and to effectively convey a complex set of information within a single message. First, the message commences with a greeting and an expression of care for other members in the group. This greeting constitutes the 'affective work' referred to above, and operates to secure the attention of group members. Second, by separating this opening from the next part of the message, Ravi invites the reader to linger on the expression of affection contained within the greeting. In this way, chunking allows users some control over the pace of the exchange, which can shape the meaning and effectiveness of the message. When we read a message that has been 'chunked', we tend to imagine that the sender is speaking to us slowly, and taking care to pause at important moments. Third, Ravi arranges the 'chunks' according to the type of information they convey; each chunk constitutes a different quality of utterance. The first is a greeting and expression of care, the second contains information about medications and their side effects, in the third Ravi shares information about their social life, in the fourth they ask group members to share information about vitamin C, before returning to the 'affective' in the final farewell message.

In the WhatsApp group chat set up to manage communications about this book, we also used utterance chunking to control the pace of messages in which we conveyed complex information across different time zones about daily work plans, as we were trying to meet tight deadlines. Our use of chunking supports Baxter's argument that chunking can be used to enhance the effectiveness of a message containing complex information. Chunking can operate as dot points, to break up different elements of the message, and encourages the receiver to pause and linger on each different element, which aids understanding. In other words, chunking alters the possibilities of what can be conveyed in a WhatsApp message:

> Emma 6:34am: I'm still working on the conclusion
> Emma 6:35am: to chapter five I mean
> Emma 6:57am: Haven't quite finished the analysis bit
> Emma 6:58am: Got to get going to work and got a meeting til your time noon
> Emma 6:58am: will work on it a bit more til your time noon til one and then after your time three pm
> Emma's WhatsApp book group chat, 2023

Scholarship has also shown how texting on WhatsApp often functions as a 'next step' for relationships that are initially forged on dating apps. Broeker (2021) shows how, among dating app users, the invitation to shift the conversation to WhatsApp is commonly understood to signal an interest in forging greater intimacy. According to Broeker, WhatsApp is positioned as a 'private' space as distinct from the publicness of dating sites, conceived of as 'the internet'. One research participant said, 'Like it feels different, you know, it becomes this really, like, taking the next step. You know, like now you're part of, like, my, you know, like we went from like the anonymity of the internet into like my private

WhatsApp' (Broeker, 2021, pp. 11–12). Emma's experience on dating apps affirms this, and also attests to WhatsApp's stickiness, in contrast to the messaging function of dating apps. In her experience, people often invite her to move the conversation off the dating app and onto WhatsApp by asking: 'Can we chat on WhatsApp? I'm hardly ever here...'. This is in contrast to WhatsApp, which users check into on a regular basis to keep in touch with friends, family and lovers.

Voice and video calls

Texting is an important element of WhatsApp use, but reports clearly demonstrate that text messaging has not replaced the need for voice calls and video calls. These features were introduced for one-on-one chats in 2015 and 2016 respectively, and in 2018 they were made available for Group chat. In 2018, WhatsApp announced that its users were spending 'over 2 billion minutes on calls per day', and in 2021, the platform said that they had seen 'significant increases in people calling one another on WhatsApp, often for long conversations'. On New Years Eve in 2020, WhatsApp broke the record for the most calls ever made in a single day with 1.4 billion voice and video calls. Throughout 2020, video calling on WhatsApp 'more than doubled' in some countries, reflecting the need for more intimate connection with loved ones during the global pandemic (Meta Newsroom, 24 April 2020).

Voice and video calls fulfil a fundamental need for WhatsApp users, especially among migrant and diasporic communities that live far away from their countries of birth, where they still have close ties with family and friends. Ariadna, for example, maintains fortnightly video group calls via WhatsApp with her sister, dad and brother. She also reported making video calls with her mum and aunty, and with friends in Barcelona. What these video calls afford her – a sense of connection, of being part of her loved ones' everyday lives despite the distance – could not be replaced by just texting with them.

Similarly, most of Ariadna's Colombian friends living in Brisbane or Amelia's partner, who lives with her in Sydney, also maintain regular video calls with their family members living in Bogotá, Girardot and Mérida. Emma, who lives in Kuala Lumpur, uses WhatsApp to call her mum in Melbourne every Sunday, even though they have usually been texting throughout the week and often don't have much news to add. For her, the voice call affords a sense of comfort and proximity that is absent from text exchanges.

Audio messages

Voice messaging is another important element of users' communicative repertoires on WhatsApp. In 2013, WhatsApp introduced voice messaging, a feature that was already offered by competitors WeChat and LINE. Around 2018, news articles began to appear calling attention to the rising popularity of voice messaging for interpersonal communication (Fernando, 2018; Pierce, 2018). As Pierce notes, voice messaging can bring back some of the 'warmth and humanity' that is absent from text messages. They also convey that voice messaging is more time efficient than texting, and less intrusive than a phone call. 'When someone calls you, typically they have no idea whether you are available to chat, or whether they are crashing into the middle of your day like a mariachi band arriving at your table' (Pierce, 2018; see also Sykes, 2018). WhatsApp frames the utility of voice messaging in similar terms:

> Voice messages have made it quick and easy for people to have more expressive conversations. Showing emotion or excitement through voice is more natural than text, and in many situations, voice messages are the preferred form of communication on WhatsApp.[2]

According to the WhatsApp blog, 7 billion voice messages are sent on the platform daily.[3] Most existing research on audio messaging examines its role in WhatsApp-based political campaigning, including misinformation, as will be explored in chapter 4 (Kischinhevsky et al., 2020; Maros et al., 2021; Pasquetto et al., 2022). Less attention has been accorded to the important role audio messaging plays in everyday relationships, such as those with friends and family. Ariadna prefers to leave audio messages for her friends in Barcelona because a voice recording affords expression of internal emotional states – the sound of laughter, the timbre of an utterance, etc. – and can serve as a better tool for securing intimacy. Ariadna has been maintaining 'slow conversation' (as she calls it) with her friend Marta via WhatsApp since she moved to Australia in 2015. Marta does not like to video or voice call, and they decided to send each other voice recordings with life updates, some of which feel almost like podcasts, lasting 15 or 20 minutes. Ariadna also sends and receives voice recordings to and from other friends, but with Marta this practice has become a ritual in their friendship. Amelia's partner, Paulina, also shares long audio updates with her friends in Mexico, which, like Ariadna, she refers to as 'podcasts'. Her best friend, a musician, often sings her updates to Paulina rather than 'speaking' them, indicating the novel expressive forms audio messaging allows.

Our interviews with users show that they find audio messaging a useful way to send a message while completing other tasks, as the anecdote from Ainin (Interview, 6/2/21) shows. In an interview with our Research Assistant, Gabriel, she said: 'When I'm very, like, busy, I don't really have time to text, so I will be like voice note instead'. Similarly, when Gabriel asked Albreda if she uses voice notes, she said:

> Yes, yes definitely I do. I do. I use voice notes on a daily basis. If I'm too lazy to type I'll just click the voice notes button and say whatever I have to say, and I feel like voice notes are so much easier because I don't have to type and all. It's just like one tap and the other person gets my message, so I use voice notes on a daily basis.
> Albreda, Kuala Lumpur, 2021

Sending voice messages not only enables users to convey emotion more effectively, but also to foreground different literacies and rhetorical abilities. Audio messaging does not distinguish those who can spell and punctuate properly from those who can't, and it makes it easier for people to communicate in other languages when their autocorrect is set to English, or in a language that they can speak, but cannot write. This is the case for Albreda, who is from Malaysia, which is a multiethnic and multilingual country where many ethnic Indians are fluent Tamil speakers, but not literate in Tamil script, because at school they only learned to read and write in English. In Albreda's case, the audio-messaging function enabled her to send messages in Tamil to her Tamil-speaking family members:

> **Gabriel:** On WhatsApp, in general, do you communicate in different languages, or is it just mainly and purely English?
> **Albreda:** Mainly it's English because my keyboard is in English, we speak in English, my autocorrect is in English, so mainly it's English. Ninety percent is in English. Then, I speak in Bahasa sometimes, Bahasa Malaysia, because we are all Malaysian right? You know how Malaysians speak and all. So yes, I speak in BM sometimes, and I also speak in Tamil. With Tamil I can't type it out and all, so I send a voice note to my parents, we speak Tamil at home, so I send voice notes and all. So, it's just English, Malay, and Tamil, mostly English. Ninety percent of the time it's English.
>
> Albreda, Kuala Lumpur, 2021

Stickers and memes

In the early years of WhatsApp, people could communicate in groups via text, images, videos and emoji. Conversation, though, was a bit messy: groups were quickly flooded with too many messages and common conversational features like the @mention and hashtags did not work the same way they did on other social media. Under Meta's ownership, WhatsApp introduced stickers (including animated stickers that are similar to GIFs) on 25 October 2018. When WhatsApp introduced stickers, it framed the new feature as an expressive shortcut that made 'communicating with friends and family ... easy and fun' and to 'help you share your feelings in a way that you can't always express with words'.[4] The blog announced the launch of an in-house sticker pack, and a set of APIs and interfaces enabling third-party developers to create stickers for the platform. Two years later, animated stickers were 'one of the fastest growing ways people communicated on WhatsApp, with billions sent every day'.[5] Ever since, the platform has partnered with different organizations and artists to create sticker packs to promote various topics, from vaccination during the COVID-19 pandemic (a partnership with the World Health Organization) to supporting women from Asia and the Pacific Islands (a collaboration with illustrator Gracia Lam).

Stickers are not specific to WhatsApp but are a feature of most mobile instant messaging platforms, such that unique sticker repertoires often define a mobile instant messaging platform. Steinberg (2020) argues that the genesis of Instant Messaging sticker culture can be traced to the Japanese platform LINE (addressed in chapter 1), which successfully monetized stickers to the point that a whole industry involving third-party apps and instructional manuals emerged around LINE stickers. Stickers have not been the money spinner for WhatsApp that they have been for LINE and other competing platforms, but anecdotal evidence and research reveals a rich culture of sticker making and sticker sharing by users, showing how the stickers are distinct from emojis, which cannot be manipulated by ordinary users. Indeed, researchers have pointed out that stickers are a genre of text that is distinct from emojis, in both form and function. Emojis belong to a set developed by Unicode and are not manipulable by ordinary users (Ohashi et al., 2017). They are iconic representations that refer to emotional states, actions or events. They are small and typically used to enhance or augment textual utterances, rather than stand alone, such that some of our research participants deemed replying with 'emoji only' a transgression of the norms of civil conversation.

> [R]eplying with emoji only, I don't agree to people replying with emoji only. There should be at least some text, or at least some things.
>
> Ainin, Kuala Lumpur, 2021

Stickers differ from emojis because they are bigger, and are typically sent as standalone messages. But like emojis, many stickers rely, for their efficacy, on the fact that they are widely recognized and have a meaning that is widely shared, and this shared quality makes them memetic in nature. At the same time, users can manipulate or create stickers using third-party apps, and this means that, unlike emojis, stickers lend themselves to contextualization and individualization.

During the height of the COVID-19 pandemic in Oman, WhatsApp users created and shared stickers as a way of responding to the management of the pandemic by the country's leaders. Al Zidjaly (2022) shows how stickers reflected the local context and conditions: they depicted Oman's leader and mediated the linguistic diversity of the country, as captions were written in formal Arabic, Omani dialect and 'reverse Arabizi' (English words written in Arabic script). Omanis used stickers to express dissent, poking fun at the leaders, and to highlight their own frustration. Al Zidjaly refers to them as 'lament memes' and argues that by creating and sharing them, ordinary users empowered themselves to participate in the management of the pandemic, and to socially construct it.

Al Zidjaly does not detail the processes involved in creating and sharing stickers, but anecdotal evidence points to sticker collecting as an important dimension of WhatsApp use, especially among older adults. Stickers can be saved and collected as 'favourites' which become accessible by clicking the star icon within the WhatsApp sticker function, and then reshared when the time is right. A quick Google search brings up a variety of sticker-making apps, and some of our research participants identified the ability to customize stickers on WhatsApp as one of the reasons they favoured it over Telegram:

> **Gabriel:** What features of WhatsApp do you like?
> **Ainin:** The stickers! I would say right now it's the stickers, because we can customize our own stickers, where Telegram cannot.
> Ainin, Kuala Lumpur, 2021

In Spain and in some Latin American countries, people use stickers to joke about WhatsApp's technical affordances and common user practices on the app. Sometimes the person that adds you to a group might be your friend, neighbour or colleague, which makes some people reluctant to exit these groups, especially because exiting leaves a trace: other groups members can see a message that says '[name of the contact] left' (see figure 3.2). This has generated user memetic engagements precisely because leaving groups without a previous warning is common, to which members can respond by making fun of this move which is sometimes perceived as passive aggressive (Staples, 2022).

There is, for example, a sticker of Jesus Christ which people use to respond to instances when someone deletes a message in a group, leaving a trace which is visible to other members. These stickers typically say: 'Jesus knows what the message you just deleted said' (see figure 3.3). To make fun of messages being sent in a group, and read by its members but not answered, people also use a sticker showing the double tick blue read receipt with the accompanying sentence: 'your message was successfully ignored' (see figure 3.3).

Other uses of stickers speak to the culture of WhatsApp but also respond to news cycles, such as when Spain's former

Everyday Uses of WhatsApp

Figure 3.2: Artist's impression of a group chat interface showing a notification that a user has left the group. Art provided by Phoebe Tan.

Prime Minister, Mariano Rajoy, was ousted in a no-confidence vote in 2018 and people sent jokes about Mariano Rajoy having left personal WhatsApp groups. In fact, at that time, various online resources were created to show users how to set up the WhatsApp joke (Manzhirova, 2018). But stickers do not always serve as light-hearted examples of ordinary users 'punching up', or simply sharing benign jokes. Matamoros-Fernández (2020) shows how the playful overtones of stickers can serve to normalize images that are harmful because they perpetuate racist stereotypes. She studied a meme that is popular in Spain and Latin America, called 'El Negro de WhatsApp' (the meme is platform specific, and therefore provides a good example of platform vernacular). The meme involves an image of a Black man, with an exposed oversized penis, who appears when users are 'tricked' into opening another image.

98 Everyday Uses of WhatsApp

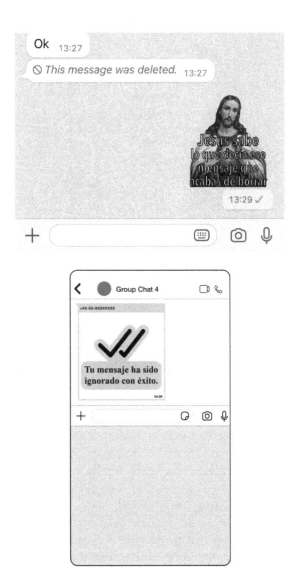

Figure 3.3: Artist's impression of a sticker showing Jesus Christ with the accompanying sentence: "Jesus knows what your deleted message said", and a sticker used to joke about messages that your group members ignore, which shows the double tick blue read receipt with the accompanying sentence: "your message was successfully ignored." Art provided by Phoebe Tan.

As Matamoros-Fernández argues, the meme exemplifies 'the transformation of media to further age-old racist stereotypes and the denigration of individuals by turning their concerns into caricatures' (Matamoros-Fernández, 2020).

Public display

The dynamics of self-presentation work has been important to scholarship on social media such as Instagram, where self-conscious exhibition of the self plays a large role (Leaver et al., 2020). Scholarship on WhatsApp has been less concerned with the ways users construct identities for public display because opportunities for such display are more limited and less prominent on WhatsApp. Rather than focusing on the ways users present themselves for public display, much of the research on WhatsApp focuses on the conversational element of the platform, and its implications for civic participation, language change and social ties. But opportunities for public display are not entirely absent on WhatsApp, and in this section we consider two features that offer such opportunities: statuses and profile pictures. The examples of public display discussed here provide evidence for our argument that WhatsApp is an intricate socio-technical system that interlaces the public and the private in complex ways.

Statuses and profile pictures

WhatsApp has included a status feature since its inception. This enables users to add 139 characters of text or emojis to their user information through editing in Settings. As we discussed in chapter 1, in February 2017 WhatsApp announced that it was doing away with this feature and replacing it with stories (called statuses, but akin to Snapchat or Instagram stories), which could be images or text, and which are accessed by a user's contacts by clicking the 'status' button. These statuses disappear after 24 hours. WhatsApp restored the original status function a month later, owing to user backlash, which we recall below (again highlighting, as we did in chapter 2, how user demands can drive platform re-design) but retained the stories-like feature:

> **Gabriel:** Do you wonder, or do you understand, why WhatsApp has stories?
> **Ainin:** I don't really, no. Why do they need a story for? I don't know.
>
> Ainin, Kuala Lumpur, 2021

> **Gabriel:** What features of WhatsApp do you not understand, if any? Like you wonder why it is on WhatsApp?
> **Amanda:** I think the story is one of them. Facebook has it, Instagram has it, and Twitter has it now as well, so for me I think the primary use of WhatsApp is texting people so I don't see why there is a need for a story feature even though I do use it very rarely.
>
> Amanda, Kuala Lumpur, 2021

However, the original status feature has been heartily embraced by users, and studies of the feature point to the various ways it has been appropriated. These studies show how the status feature has become infused with linguistic devices and power relations that pre-exist the feature, showing how rich platform vernaculars emerge from simple features such as statuses. For example, Bashir-Badmus (2018) examined how different types of statuses were shaped by gender and found that men and women posted differently, with men tending to be more assertive. In their study of Spanish users, Maiz-Arévalo (2021) found that older users are not at all appropriative, and tended to rely on automatically generated statuses (e.g., 'Hallo there! I'm using WhatsApp', 'Busy', 'Available', etc.), but that younger users prefer to generate their own. Maiz-Arévalo studied these self-generated statuses, and found they could be grouped into different categories, including inspirational, emotional, critical, implicit (meant for close friends) and humorous. Similarly, Rababah (2020) also identified 'genres' of statuses, which they categorized as religious, social, personal, romantic, political, national and sport-oriented. The emergence of such genres shows how people adopt and adapt the features of WhatsApp to build and project their identities to a 'public' constituted by users who are in their contact list, including businesses they interact with.

The profile picture is another feature of WhatsApp that enables users to present a coherent 'self' to their contacts at large. The way they do so also highlights how users extend features beyond the original intention of the designers. On WhatsApp, the profile picture feature is bounded by a circular line, suggesting it was designed with headshots in mind, perhaps as a verification tool. But in the course of everyday use, the profile picture has become much more than that. It is not uncommon for users to adopt profile pictures that show their bodies and face to enable recognition, but many users also use it to obscure their identity (using images of cartoon characters or superheroes), or to display elements of their identity that do not involve bodily display. Udo's (2018) study of South African users shows how they resorted to the profile feature in order to identify their ideological affiliations, and others used it to register political protest. This too, like the status feature discussed above, shows how people draw features of the platform into their efforts to construct a coherent 'self' and project it to their contacts at large.

Conclusion

In the Introduction to this book, we discussed how the widespread uptake of WhatsApp produces network effects, which refers to the correlation between the number of people using a platform and its value. In practical terms, network effects are at play when a communication platform becomes the primary site for a user to communicate with a wide range of contacts: a kind of one-stop shop. They offer users the convenience of having a single locus from which to engage in a variety of exchanges and relationships, including friendly, familial, professional, commercial and intimate ones. Users then experience the prospect of shifting to a new, technically superior platform, albeit with a smaller network, as an inconvenience.

In this chapter, we have argued that, while the concept of network effects can partly explain WhatsApp's continued dominance of the mobile messaging landscape, it glosses over the ways users appropriate the features of the platform as its network grows in size and complexity. We have adopted the term 'platform vernacular' from Gibbs et al. (2015) to describe the appropriations described herein. 'Network effects' aids understanding of how and why WhatsApp serves as a convenient communication tool, and by extension why leaving it could be inconvenient, but 'platform vernaculars' help account for its stickiness: the enjoyment and pleasure people derive from using the platform, which keeps them 'glued' to it. As we have shown in this chapter, WhatsApp is much more than simply a 'one-stop-shop' offering users the convenience of a single site for communicating with a range of contacts. It is also a cultural space, moulded and shaped by users to accommodate humour, creativity, intimacy and care. Network effects enhance value because the size of the network correlates with convenience; it ensures that people rely on the platform to maintain their personal stake in social networks. User appropriation adds value because it is what enables users to invest in social networks expressively, and with agency.

We have examined everyday uses of WhatsApp, and limited our focus to those everyday uses that take place between ordinary users on the app. We have excluded from the discussion consideration of everyday engagements with news, governments, corporations and among activists as these have been explored in chapter 2 and will also be the focus of chapter 4. In this chapter, we have instead documented the everyday user practices that constitute WhatsApp as a 'living room' or 'bedroom' where private one-on-one exchanges, as well as private or semi-public exchanges with family groups, neighbourhood groups and support groups, take place. The chapter has highlighted the various practices and meanings that arise from the variety of historical and cultural contexts in which WhatsApp has been taken up. In the next chapter, we explore how these variations play out in WhatsApp's 'town square', via its use by pro-democracy activists, journalists and news organizations, and political parties and governments. We explore how tensions arising from such use delineate two possibilities for WhatsApp as a public forum, one of which highlights its significance to civic participation, and another which highlights its manipulation by powerful actors (political parties and governments) with outcomes which are claimed to threaten democracy.

4
WhatsApp Publics

On 8 May 2018, the *Barisan Nasional* coalition government, the longest-serving elected government in the world at that time, was defeated in Malaysia's 14th general election. One explanation for their defeat was the role of activists and citizen journalists who, for years, had used blogs and social media to foster an 'opposition playground' in a context of media censorship and repression (Cheong, 2021). Government attempts to silence these voices after the 2013 election, by arresting citizens speaking out on social media[1] (primarily Facebook and Twitter), only served to embolden activists, who turned to encrypted platforms like WhatsApp to shield their communications from state surveillance (Johns, 2020). In interviews with Amelia in 2016, activists described WhatsApp as a safe space for coordinating and discussing politics within an ecosystem of private and semi-public, end-to-end encrypted groups. WhatsApp's large group sizes, Broadcast list function and web and desktop applications also helped activists to mobilize and coordinate large numbers of volunteers. Two interviewees noted these safety and mass coordination affordances:

> I think [WhatsApp] was somewhat safer ... safe for me to discuss politics, rather than discussing it publicly ... because there are always people watching even if you've set your settings to private.
> Hai Yang, activist, Kuala Lumpur, 2016

> It's one of our primary communication methods internally, for staff and committee members, but also with our partners ... we have a whole bunch of groups because each campaign

will have a new group. The last bi-elections, we formed WhatsApps groups for the volunteers so if we need to disseminate information, or mobilize people for certain things, it's just a matter of mass communicating through WhatsApp.

Billy, campaign manager, Kuala Lumpur, 2016

Activist uses of WhatsApp, and descriptions of the platform as a safe space, were a telling finding. But in follow-up interviews in 2018, mere months after the 14th General Election, a new narrative was emerging. Activists still saw value in WhatsApp for coordinating and organizing but they felt the technology to be less safe than previously. Informants expressed anxiety about the volume of 'fake news' and misinformation that circulated on WhatsApp private and semi-public groups (Johns & Cheong, 2021). In one example, an informant told Amelia that doctored photos of politicians were being shared through her WhatsApp groups in the lead up to the election, while two other informants showed her a chain mail that had been forwarded many times through friends, family, and work groups during the campaign period (see figure 4.1). One of these 'chain letter' messages insinuated that the government were in 'secret talks' and would announce that the Prime Minister would be standing down to try to save votes for the government. In another, the message warned citizens not to celebrate if the opposition won as this could create conditions for government-paid thugs to stir up violence, both claims that were later proven to be unfounded.

These examples foreshadow the key themes of this chapter, which continues chapter 3's exploration of the role of WhatsApp in people's everyday lives, but shifts the focus to consider how WhatsApp affords users and organizations opportunities for security, coordination, news-sharing and broadcasting. We also reflect on the technical and social dimensions of WhatsApp that have shaped public communication practices and misuse, attracting negative global, media and policy attention. In using the term 'public', we draw attention to the way WhatsApp, though often considered to

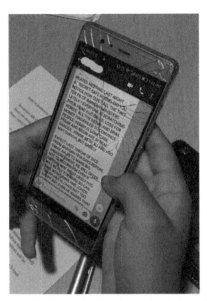

Figure 4.1: Photograph taken by Amelia (July, 2018) of an informant's family group chat, and a chain mail message containing misinformation, which circulated prior to Malaysian 14th General Election.

be for private chat, has features that allow it to become more like a broadcast tool and public forum that plays an important role in the formation of public opinion.

As Gillespie (2018) claims, one of the defining features of platforms is the way that they call publics or communities into being by providing tools for users to create and share content, not just with known contacts, but with strangers. In so doing, platforms create opportunities for public expression and participation that can have far-reaching influence on public discourse, for better or worse. In the case of WhatsApp, this is mostly seen in countries where WhatApp groups' URLs are shared on the open web and used as public discussion forums where anyone with the link can join to discuss topics of interest. Yet WhatsApp's progressive increase of group size, which allows for the creation of 'closed' and encrypted groups of up to 1,024 people, and more than this with the new Communities feature, also facilitates interactions among strangers and makes the sharing of problematic content difficult to address. One of the consequences of this more 'public' nature of WhatsApp has been that the platform has had to put mechanisms in place to moderate content, a definitional characteristic of platforms (Gillespie, 2018). To avoid liability and scandal, WhatsApp, like other more public-facing platforms, governs use via its Terms of Service[2] and community guidelines,[3] which the platform enforces in a rather opaque manner (Gillespie et al., 2020).

These more public uses of WhatsApp that have required the platform to moderate content allow us to imagine WhatsApp as the 'digital equivalent to the town square', to use Zuckerberg's metaphorical description. Zuckerberg used this metaphor in 2019 to refer to Instagram and Facebook, while he described WhatsApp as being more like a 'living room' for private, interpersonal communication (Matamoros-Fernàndez et al., 2019; Zuckerberg, 2019a). In this chapter we show how this latter description does not hold true, especially if we look at how WhatsApp is used by its largest user bases in the Global South.

Continuing our examination of the social dimension of WhatsApp's platformization, we begin the chapter by examining how activists have used WhatsApp as far more than a chat app since its early beginnings. We draw from our research with activists in Malaysia and other examples from Spain and Latin America to illustrate how WhatsApp became an essential part of activist repertoires by offering options to switch between private and public forms of address, affording safety in contexts of state repression and censorship of information. We then turn our attention to how WhatsApp has transformed institutional practices of journalism and news-making, with its broadcasting and media-sharing capabilities (facilitated by media share button plug-in and the forwarding function). These features have facilitated WhatsApp's positioning as the third largest gateway to news and a major platform for journalists and news organizations to reach new and established audiences (Newman et al., 2018). The introduction of the Broadcast list function, the Group invite link and the Forward function have called 'publics' into being and transformed WhatsApp into a platform that shapes public discourse and encourages civic participation among a broad cross-section of users, from activists to the non-politically engaged (Vermeer et al., 2021).

Finally, we turn attention to the ways politicians and their teams have misappropriated WhatsApp's capabilities for public formation and mass coordination to manipulate publics and gain electoral advantage. They do so by circulating disinformation that, due to limited moderation, cannot be traced back to the source (Banaji et al., 2019; Baulch et al., 2022; Evangelista & Bruno, 2019). This, we argue, contributes to 'information disorder' (Wardle & Derakhshan, 2017), producing toxic environments where hate and misinformation circulate unchecked. Further, we focus on the way that misuse of WhatsApp's encrypted public and private group infrastructure has also allowed everyday users to circulate hoaxes and rumour with little oversight. The chapter concludes with a reflection on the chorus of contesting social actors (regulators, governments, law enforcement) who have forced Meta to make design changes, and are continuing to call for more regulation to limit misuse and restore public confidence in democratic institutions.

Activism

Activists' use of WhatsApp has been well documented. As early as 2014, activists incorporated WhatsApp into their communication practices, with one of the earliest examples being the Iranian government's decision, in 2014, to block WhatsApp to prevent activists using the platform (Khazraee & Losey, 2016; Pang & Woo, 2020). Most often, WhatsApp has been used for activism in contexts where the mechanisms guaranteeing democracy – freedom of political expression and media freedoms – are not available or are suppressed by governments (Khazraee & Losey, 2016; Lee & Ting, 2015; Pang & Woo, 2020; Santos & Faure, 2018; Treré, 2015). Even before the introduction of end-to-end encryption, WhatsApp's private and semi-closed groups made it attractive to organizers seeking an 'intimate and controlled' communication environment to connect with other activists and volunteers (Gil de Zúñiga et al., 2021, p. 201). Some activists have also pointed to WhatsApp's reliability and flexibility as a reason for using the platform, citing the ability to switch between devices and locations, and coordinate volunteers from their computer (using WhatsApp web and desktop versions) or smartphone (Milan & Barbosa, 2020).

Use of WhatsApp in Mexico's #YoSoy132 movement (Treré, 2015) and Spain's 15M movement (Treré, 2020) provide a good illustration of how the platform's privacy affordances and semi-closed design have made it a preferred platform for activists' internal communication practices.[4] As a result, WhatsApp has been described by some digital media scholars as a 'social media backstage' (Treré, 2015, p. 902; see also Chagas, 2022). The use of sociologist Erving Goffman's theatrical metaphor of 'frontstage' and 'backstage' clearly locates WhatsApp, in this context, as a private domain (or 'backstage') where activists can connect, plan and coordinate away from the 'official lights' of the digital frontstage (Twitter, YouTube and Facebook) (Treré, 2015, p. 911). For the #YoSoy132 activists, WhatsApp functioned as a 'digital comfort zone' where 'personal and intimate' communication practices helped foster a sense of solidarity, care, collective identity and purpose. WhatsApp also allowed activists to decompress from 'public-facing' communications by encouraging practices of 'ludic activism' – referring to the sharing of memetic media[5] and other playful communication practices that relieved them from the constant pressures of frontstage audience management (Treré, 2015, p. 907).

Scholars have consistently pointed to WhatsApp's semi-closed architecture and private groups as features that enhance user feelings of safety, intimacy, trust and control. This can be compared to feed-scrolling platforms such as Facebook and Twitter where algorithms nudge users towards new social connections, and where anxiety around 'context collapse' (boyd, 2010) can produce worry and 'self-censorship' (Marwick & boyd, 2011, p. 125). This has led to claims that civic and political discussion can become 'chilled' on more public-facing platforms (Gil de Zúñiga et al., 2021; Goh et al., 2019; Johns & Cheong, 2019; Kalogeropoulos, 2021; Swart et al., 2019; Valeriani & Vaccari, 2018; Velasquez et al., 2021).

At the same time, WhatsApp is not just a platform for 'backstage' communication practices. The functionality of Groups, the Broadcast list and increased user controls for admins (as documented in chapter 2) have shaped WhatsApp into a platform where communities can come together to discuss issues, and where admins can coordinate and mobilize publics rapidly. WhatsApp has been used as a mobilization tool by activists in Brazil, owing to its reach and penetration, with 96 per cent of the population being on WhatsApp (Milan & Barbosa, 2020; Pereira & Bojzuk, 2018; Valenzuela et al., 2021). Its media-sharing functions and public group capabilities have also made it the number one venue for citizens to find and discuss news (Milan & Barbosa, 2020; Newman et al., 2018). The absence of algorithms mediating conversations has made it a unique platform for mobilizing social and political action. Describing how a private WhatsApp group called *#Unidos Contra o Golpe* (United Against the Coup) emerged to contest the impeachment of former Brazilian President Dilma Rousseff, Milan and Barbosa (2020) reveal that the absence of algorithmic mediation allowed activism to emerge 'organically' with the sharing of expressive content such as memes, audios and videos acting as the prompt for activism rather than strategic, coordinated behaviour.

Expressive and 'connective' modes of activism were also observed by Amelia, who, in 2019, joined a private Malaysian activist group on WhatsApp. She observed the ebb and flow of interactions in the group, where all members were listed as administrators and responsible for collectively organizing and managing the group's affairs. This ranged from: social interactions and the sharing of personal and expressive content among the group (e.g., personal photos of family members, activist 'inspo' memes); the creation of joint press statements in solidarity with workers and trade union groups; and sharing calls to action and content with other related activist groups. Over time, this blending of private and semi-public communication practices consolidated group bonds and developed the values and focus of the group's activity.

After 2016 there was a further shift towards the use of WhatsApp by activists in Malaysia (Johns, 2020; Johns & Cheong, 2021), which some of Amelia's informants linked to Meta's decision to add end-to-end encryption to all individual and group chats and calls. As discussed in chapter 2, the adoption of the Open Whisper protocol endorsed by Edward Snowden (Hintz et al., 2019) persuaded many activists around the world to view WhatsApp as a safe communication channel. Company announcements sought to endorse this view, claiming that privacy was now 'coded' into WhatsApp's DNA and 'oppressive regimes' would not be able to read users' private conversations. Such declarations did help restore some trust in the platform despite its purchase by Meta, whose business model for its other platforms is dependent on ad-driven revenue acquired by selling user data. In interviews with Malaysian activists, informants stressed the importance of WhatsApp's encryption in the context of heavy government surveillance of the digital 'frontstage' (Twitter and Facebook). One informant believed that encryption enhanced trust that information was now safe from the government, although they retained lingering concerns about Meta's intentions.

At the time they were all saying, 'Oh Facebook's going to buy WhatsApp, we're all going to be screwed, they're going to suck in our phone numbers and our profiles against our will and we'll have to delete everything manually.' So, I was freaking out ... except our worst fears have not come to pass somehow and they've also introduced encryption. So, we are at least safe from the government, but not necessarily from Facebook.
> Julian, activist, Kuala Lumpur, 2016

While in many contexts and for less surveilled social groups the affordances of encryption do not carry the same weight, for many activists in Malaysia and elsewhere, end-to-end encryption quickly became a game-changer (Milan & Barbosa, 2020). Notwithstanding scepticism from digital media scholars who have long argued that the introduction of encryption on WhatsApp was performative, and did not stop WhatsApp collecting user metadata that could be shared with governments and law enforcement (Santos & Faure, 2018), research has shown that it enhances perceptions of safety in discussing controversial topics (Kalogeropoulos, 2018).

Despite this, some activists that Amelia interviewed in 2016 urged their activist friends to move to Telegram, owing to their belief it was more secure. But they quickly discovered that WhatsApp's popularity made it too sticky to leave:

> Most of my activist friends are on WhatsApp ... I already tell them Telegram is better, more secure, but a lot of them refuse to turn to Telegram because I believe it's also affected by the crowd ... WhatsApp is more famous here.
> Hai Yang, activist, Kuala Lumpur, 2016

In the next section we examine how WhatsApp's stickiness derives in part from the capacity to share news and information within the context of everyday conversations. This feature of WhatsApp has allowed it to evolve into a dominant platform for news distribution in the countries where its user base is largest (including Brazil, India, Indonesia and

Malaysia), which has in turn had a transformative effect on media organizations and the business of news.

News organizations and journalism

In 2015, two years after the launch of the WhatsApp media share button, the Reuters Digital News Report dedicated five pages to document the decline of print news consumption, and the rise of consumption via social media. The report found Facebook to be a dominant source of news around the world, but it also noted that 'outside the US' WhatsApp was fast becoming a key gateway to news, with 27 per cent of people in Spain, and 34 per cent in Brazil, using the platform for news. Brands and corporations also started adding WhatsApp share buttons to their sites to capitalize on WhatsApp's growing user base, and its growth into a content distribution platform (Newman et al., 2015, p. 13). Successive Reuters news reports noted the continued growth of WhatsApp as a gateway to news in many countries. In 2018 the report identified that WhatsApp had become the third most used platform to receive, read and share news globally, and stated that 'WhatsApp use for news has almost tripled since 2014 and has overtaken Twitter in importance in many countries' (Newman et al., 2018, pp. 12–13).

The regions where WhatsApp has become most commonly used for discussing and sharing news are: Kenya (where 61% of the population reads news on WhatsApp), Nigeria (60%), Brazil (41%), Colombia (40%), Indonesia (54%), India (51%) and Malaysia (47%). In Europe, Spain leads the way with 31 per cent of the country using WhatsApp for news (Newman et al., 2018). The reasons for the popular uptake of WhatsApp for news vary across geographic region and context. As discussed in chapter 1, the rollout of Free Basics in many countries in the Global South – which transformed WhatsApp into the default communication platform for users – could provide one explanation for its popularity as a news source.

Activists' and ordinary users' sense of privacy and safety on WhatsApp, cited above, provide another explanation. In contexts of heavy media censorship and restrictions on free speech, research shows that people are more reluctant to discuss news and contentious political issues on more open social networks (Kalogeropoulos, 2018, p. 53). Taking this into account, WhatsApp provides an environment where news can be shared and discussed in private, with close personal contacts (Gil de Zúñiga et al., 2021; Kalogeropoulos, 2018). Other explanations focus on the convenience and social affordances of WhatsApp, which are better at facilitating and maintaining continuous discussion of news. In these explanations, the 'always on' nature of WhatsApp (Matassi et al., 2019) enabled by the affordances of mobility and multimodality that it shares with many mobile instant messaging applications, allows users to interact with the platform on their phone, on the move and at any time of day. This flexibility is enhanced by the availability of the Forward function, meaning information sharing, as well as political talk, become a part of an uninterrupted stream of social interaction and daily conversation (Valeriani & Vaccari, 2018, p. 1716; Velasquez et al., 2021), as introduced in chapter 2.

News and discussion also take place in large, 'public' groups, where admins can publish links to groups on the open web (websites, blogs and social media pages) inviting a larger audience or 'public' to join based on the topic (Caetano et al., 2018; Casaes & Córdova, 2019). While many public WhatsApp groups unite people around social or leisure activities – for example, support for a sporting club – studies have revealed the high prevalence of news and politically oriented discussion groups in countries where WhatsApp has the largest penetration. This includes India, Brazil and parts of Africa (Caetano et al., 2018; Milan & Barbosa, 2020; Nizaruddin, 2021; Resende et al., 2019; Tapsell, 2018). These groups more closely resemble online forums or social networks, fostering different communication practices to private groups.

Discussing how public groups work in Nigeria, Cheeseman et al. (2020) claim that, typically, public WhatsApp groups are established by organizations rather than individuals. These may be religious organizations, professional or alumni associations and social movements. In Nigeria, Brazil and India, public groups are often established and administered by members of political parties, party affiliates and campaign workers who instrumentalize these groups as a tool for mass mobilization and persuasion in election contexts (Banaji et al., 2019; Casaes & Córdova, 2019; Cheeseman et al., 2020). Research in Brazil uses the metaphor of the 'talk show' format to explain what forms of public address and communication techniques have become normalized in this context. To illustrate the metaphor, research has shown that news topics are often introduced and discussed by a 'host' while users 'listen' like an audience (Caetano et al., 2018). Nonetheless, audiences are not inactive. In Nigeria, Cheeseman et al. (2020) found that news shared in public groups travelled quickly via use of the Forward button. The typical user in this country belonged to multiple groups, including large groups with the maximum number of members (256 at the time in the year the study was published). This meant that if a single user belonged to five groups, then a message or media content could be forwarded to 1,280 people at a time. This is how information goes viral on WhatsApp where it is used as a primary news- and information-sharing channel.

Broadcasting on WhatsApp

WhatsApp Broadcast lists are a powerful way to connect news organizations and journalists with audiences, with almost all news outlets in countries such as Spain and Brazil having buttons on their websites where users can subscribe to Broadcast lists to receive news digests (also called channels or newsletters; see Bapaye & Bapaye, 2021; Boczek & Koppers, 2020, p. 127; Dodds, 2019; Gil de Zúñiga et al., 2021; Swart et al., 2019). In the UK the practice of using WhatsApp Broadcast lists to deliver news to subscribers has led to innovative practices. This may be seen in content designed to deliver news to users' pockets (or their smart watch) during their daily commute, like daily traffic alerts (Reid, 2014). Rather than oversaturating users' limited attention with constant notifications, editors have also spoken of adapting content delivery times and news notifications, developing sensitivity to new temporal rhythms of news consumption via WhatsApp:

> Limiting the number of messages to two or three alerts a day is important though ... it stops readers becoming 'desensitized' to the alert. It is not a 'bulk medium' ... so morning and evening announcements linking to the top stories have worked best. (Reid, 2014)

In Israel, Broadcast lists have been used to deliver and also monetize news for digital audiences. Journalists such as Tal Schneider have used this means of targeted public broadcasting to offer an exclusive, behind-the-scenes view into the news production process, with access being dependent on a small subscription fee. Leveraging the value placed on social reciprocity in WhatsApp groups, the subscriber channel shares 'behind the scenes' updates while also introducing novel practices where subscribers can participate in 'crowdsourced interviews with politicians and pundits' (Kligler-Vilenchik & Tenenboim, 2020, p. 265). Similar methods have been used by the *New York Times* to offer exclusive views of Pope Francis's tour of Latin America in 2015, with a subscription-based Broadcast list being used to send regular communication and news updates to its audience. Speaking of the 'experiment', Jim Yardley, the *New York Times* Rome Bureau Chief Editor, explained that as publishers increasingly look to 'external distribution platforms' to remain relevant, 'the sheer size' of WhatsApp's user base was impossible to ignore.[6]

WhatsApp Publics

The broadcasting capabilities of WhatsApp have also proven popular with governments. In 2020, as conspiracy theories and misinformation about the COVID-19 pandemic circulated on all social media, WhatsApp's reach and popularity led governments to set up WhatsApp channels (another name for Broadcast lists) to distribute official information. In Australia, as soon as the government set up a dedicated WhatsApp channel to broadcast updates on COVID-19 case numbers, Amelia subscribed. To interact with the channel and select specific updates and information, users were instructed to reply with an emoji such as a rolled-up newspaper for news, or a calculator for case numbers (see figure 4.2).

For Amelia, the channel became a simple and easy-to-use way of receiving official COVID-19 updates in a context where much of the news circulating on social media platforms,

Figure 4.2: Australian Government official Coronavirus WhatsApp channel. Screenshot taken by Amelia, 6 October 2021.

including WhatsApp, referred to information that was out of date, incomplete, confusing or possibly fabricated. In the next section of the chapter, we spend time exploring this other, darker side of WhatsApp by referring to the frequently documented use of the platform to circulate mis- and disinformation, contributing to 'information disorder' (Wardle & Derakhshan, 2017). We also consider how WhatsApp's design features have turned WhatsApp into a platform where disinformation circulates through private and public groups, and where political actors have taken advantage of WhatsApp's encryption, anonymity and limited algorithmic content moderation, to manipulate election outcomes. All of this has eroded public trust and confidence in key institutions of democracy, and has brought reckoning for Meta's design decisions.

Information disorder

'Information disorder' is a common way of understanding how the circulation of harmful content on social media platforms impacts public confidence in democracy (Wardle & Derakhshan, 2017). First coined by Wardle and Derakhshan, the term captures a worrying global trend where politicians and other social actors have used social media to spread or amplify rumour and false information with the intention to 'sow mistrust and confusion and to sharpen existing sociocultural divisions' (p. 4) and manipulate the outcomes of elections.

Policymakers, regulators and researchers concerned with the spread of mis- and disinformation[7] have more often focused their attention on open platforms such as Facebook and Twitter (Woolley & Howard, 2019). This focus has tended to overshadow the common use of encrypted messaging platforms to spread harmful content, particularly in the Global South (Gursky et al., 2022). The weaponization of WhatsApp's features that enable users to send bulk and automated messages; the use of cybertroopers or 'digital militias' (Milan & Barbosa, 2020) to amplify and spread political messaging while giving the appearance of grassroots engagement; and the exploitation of WhatsApp's multimodal features (text, video, photos, audios and memes) to spread false and harmful information using popular culture and humour are features of what we call in this book an information disorder 'playbook'. In what follows, we introduce the main elements of this playbook, and consider the implications, for users, for the democratic fabric of societies, and for Meta's ambitions to transform WhatsApp into a global communication and business platform.

Easy sharing, fast spread and encryption

One of the main reasons why WhatsApp has become a hub for harmful and misleading content is its design: information spreads fast due to the Group and Forward features, and it is difficult to moderate due to encryption. The same affordances and protections that have made WhatsApp a safe space for activists and journalists have also facilitated misuse of the platform. For example, a user might share a public news link, blog post or web page from outside WhatsApp, where information may have been doctored or taken out of context. This may initially be forwarded with the intention to deceive. Once the content finds its way into private groups, other users, believing the content's legitimacy, might forward the content on to multiple other private, public or semi-public groups with hundreds of members. Once information arrives in these WhatsApp groups, people can feel compelled to share the content for various reasons. Different sets of social norms and/or emotional or affective responses to the content of the message can influence the likelihood of users forwarding the content. For example, in studies of social norms among users believing or forwarding misinformation during the COVID-19 pandemic, trust in the contact sharing the information, the social status of the sharer (i.e., a senior member of a family or community leader) and avoidance of social conflict among close contacts is a strong predictor of whether messages are forwarded or at least remain uncorrected (Bapaye & Bapaye, 2021; Chadwick et al., 2022; Riedl et al., 2022; Tandoc et al., 2020; Varanasi et al., 2022).

Encryption also complicates content moderation on WhatsApp, making techniques such as proactive algorithmic detection of harmful content, including misinformation, more difficult, as discussed in detail in chapter 2. Further, while WhatsApp has access to behavioural metadata, the absence of content metadata complicates tracking of media to an original source (Rossini et al., 2021, p. 2435). This makes interventions around Forward limits the only tool available (Chadwick et al., 2022, pp. 9–10) to moderate content, together with giving users the ability to report messages and media, groups, accounts and communities. This content is then reviewed by paid moderators or fact checkers (Elkind et al., 2021). Encryption also makes users who spread disinformation virtually untraceable, making WhatsApp and other platforms like it a high priority for governments around the world as they seek to address the use of the platform as a 'vector for sowing misinformation' (Gursky et al., 2022, p. 1). An example of this threat is growing evidence that WhatsApp groups may shield cells that operate within larger, cross-platform disinformation operations, enabling them to traffic propaganda and hate speech from 'downstream', encrypted layers of the digital ecosystem 'upstream' into mainstream public discourse (Gursky et al., 2022, p. 2).

The limited content moderation on WhatsApp and the rapid spread of harmful content via shares and groups has played a key role in the spread of hoaxes, rumour and hate speech targeting marginalized and vulnerable communities. It has led to mob violence and lynchings, especially in India (Banaji et al., 2019) and Mexico (Martinez, 2018), where rumours of child abductions circulating through WhatsApp private groups have led to the formation of vigilante mobs and communal violence. Research during the COVID-19 pandemic also found that WhatsApp groups run by or affiliated with political parties in India have become fertile spaces for the sharing of Islamophobic memes and sentiment (Banaji et al., 2019, pp. 34–5). During the pandemic, the circulation of 'CoronaJihad' memes on public Hindutva WhatsApp groups – which included members of the Bharatiya Janata Party (BJP) – targeted and blamed Muslims for deliberately spreading the virus (Nizaruddin, 2021, p. 1103). According to the authors, the establishment of multiple, connected groups conveying this content establishes WhatsApp as a key site which sustains 'ecosystems of hate' in the country (Nizaruddin, 2021, p. 1104).

Networks of trust and political manipulation

Another main reason why harmful content thrives on WhatsApp, which we have partially touched upon in the previous section, is that information on the platform is largely spread via networks of trust (Chadwick et al., 2018). Acknowledging this, people interested in misleading, manipulating or harming via the platform have come up with tactics to make the most of WhatsApp groups' association with close, trusted contacts, manipulating this context to bulk message multiple groups without being detected by WhatsApp, which employs artificial intelligence to track down suspicious behaviour (WhatsApp, 2019).

WhatsApp first introduced machine learning systems in 2019 to detect coordinated behaviour on the platform and remove networks of accounts, but as interviews with operatives in India reveal, such interventions are not feared by teams who are effective in overcoming these restrictions (Gursky et al., 2022, p. 6). Bulk messaging on WhatsApp has been especially effective during elections in Brazil, India, Indonesia, Malaysia and Nigeria, with some commentators defining these events as 'WhatsApp elections' (Cheeseman et al., 2020; Johns, 2020; Nizaruddin, 2021). Research has documented the use of highly sophisticated hierarchies of group admins operating large, public and private WhatsApp groups 'in pyramid-like campaign team structures' (Baulch et al., 2022, p. 5). These groups are established for the sole purpose of creating content and spreading political messaging and disinformation (see also Casaes & Córdova, 2019; Chagas, 2022; Evangelista & Bruno, 2019). Paid and unpaid volunteers or 'cybertroopers' are employed within this infrastructure to amplify and spread content in a manner that is difficult to trace. In Brazil researchers found evidence of mass coordination across hundreds of public WhatsApp groups in the 2018 Brazilian general election, where the use of such methods elevated a relatively unknown, far-right political candidate, Jair Bolsonaro, to win the election (Evangelista & Bruno, 2019). Content and social network analysis of Bolsonarist WhatsApp groups revealed 'patterns of activity among members and group administrators that resemble hierarchically organized networks performing coordinated actions with a high degree of centrality' (Chagas, 2022, p. 2433). Despite WhatsApp intervening on the eve of the election to reduce the Forward limit to 20 (as it had done in India following the WhatsApp lynchings) and to remove 100,000 users found to be sending automated messages, the monitored groups remained highly active during and after the election (ibid., p. 2438).

These findings are supported by research on the Indian general election of 2019, where it has been argued that 'the production and distribution of ... misinformation and disinformation ... has become institutionalized' (Banaji et al., 2019, p. 19; see also Gursky et al., 2022; Nizaruddin, 2021). Researchers point to a 'sophisticated and well-established social infrastructure' (Banaji et al., 2019, p. 23) of WhatsApp groups coordinated by 'current and former' members of the BJP (Gursky et al., 2022, p. 5). Using this multiple group structure, content is created or sourced from data and advertising agencies and 'disseminated at high speed'. Digital rights observers in the country claim that the top trending digital topics on WhatsApp in India are invariably 'manufactured by political IT cells' (p. 6).

This level of coordination and management of WhatsApp groups by political parties was also reflected in Emma and Ariadna's research on the Indonesian election of 2019 (Baulch et al., 2022). Interviews with party operatives and 'volunteers' supporting President Jokowi's re-election campaign revealed teams running coordinated messaging on WhatsApp (Baulch et al., 2022, p. 8). These were organized into three layers of campaign organization and 'memetic persuasion', by which the light-hearted, humorous and accessible nature of memetic images was leveraged to make a well-financed and well-coordinated social media election campaign appear to emerge from the 'grass roots', rather than 'top down' (Baulch et al., 2022, p. 8). The first layer was referred to by informants as the 'white' layer. This cell distributed positive memes and campaign materials. The 'red' layer 'relied heavily on dedicated Jokowi WhatsApp support groups', which disseminated official attack campaigns. The 'black' layer comprised volunteers or 'buzzers' who created and shared memes containing misinformation. This mirrored a similar communication structure used in Nigeria's 2019 election where media centres were established to oversee content distribution in 36 Nigerian states (Cheeseman et al., 2020). The centres were coordinated by 'chapter leaders' who were only informally linked to the party-political machinery, and so had the freedom to operate independently. These networks were so crucial to the shaping of public discourse in Nigeria that informants claimed that once crafted and disseminated 'in less than 10 minutes, information can spread across the country' (p. 149).

The use of phone lists is another common tactic in the information disorder playbook. WhatsApp does not require real name identification, with users only needing a mobile number to register an account. Political operatives have exploited this design by using burner phones, international numbers and mobile phone numbers purchased via advertising firms, and data brokers, so that numbers are unable to be traced back to a registered user. There is a whole black market of these numbers also available on the web (see figure 4.3), offering '1000s of messages' and 'unlimited senders' to be used in bulk-messaging campaigns (Evangelista & Bruno, 2019; Tactical Tech, 2019). Holes in some country's privacy laws, like Brazil, further facilitate misuse of WhatsApp (Casaes & Córdova, 2019). To register a mobile number in Brazil, it must be linked to a user's tax file number. Due to lax privacy laws, however, the tax file numbers of deceased people (called *laranjas*) are 'relatively easy to obtain' (p. 6). This allows practices of mobile numbers being registered under fraudulent IDs to facilitate bulk messaging (Casaes & Córdova, 2019, p. 6).

Automated bulk messaging

One of the most effective disinformation and propaganda techniques on WhatsApp involves the use of automated messaging software to create a massive pipeline of disinformation, despite WhatsApp having mechanisms to detect this type of behaviour. While against WhatsApp's Terms

Figure 4.3: Artist's impression of advertisements on the open web selling registered phone numbers to enable mass messaging on WhatsApp. Art provided by Phoebe Tan.

of Service, companies have developed systems to send automated messages through WhatsApp. Automated bulk messaging systems allow content to be broadcast to users across multiple groups, without the need for whole teams of paid volunteers (Gursky et al., 2022, p. 7). WhatsApp has confirmed that automated messages also played a part in Jair Bolsonaro's campaign with 'up to 300,000 WhatsApp accounts' being used to automate the broadcast of disinformation and to coordinate non-reported political advertising (Casaes & Córdova, 2019, p. 6).

Research has found that automation software was developed to target a range of organically created public WhatsApp groups during the election campaign. These included diabetic discussion groups, soccer team supporters, Uber drivers and others. The software 'used algorithms that segmented group members into supporters, detractors and neutral members and defined and sent content accordingly' (Evangelista & Bruno, 2019, p. 14). Similar strategies of segmentation of WhatsApp groups into different demographics of users were also noted in the Indian election campaign, where Gursky et al. noted:

> Large numbers of WhatsApp groups ... are run by local volunteers who create groups of approximately 50–100 community members that mirror offline networks of like-minded people. Members of these groups are then targeted with messaging informed by hyper-specific data purchased from data brokers. (Gursky et al., 2022, p. 5)

This type of segmented messaging, called 'micro-targeting', has been identified on Facebook and other large social media platforms, with these platforms able to detect and respond to automated and coordinated inauthentic behaviour by removing networks of accounts. Nonetheless, the closed, end-to-end encrypted nature of WhatsApp makes detection of these strategies more difficult (Evangelista & Bruno, 2019, p. 15).

Audio messaging

A final tactic that has been employed to fuel misleading and harmful content on WhatsApp is the exploitation of cultural forms that are popular on the platform, such as memes, stickers, chain mail, short videos (Baulch et al., 2022; Cheeseman et al., 2020; Johns & Cheong, 2021; Milan & Barbosa, 2020; Tapsell, 2018) and audios (Kischinhevsky et al., 2020). The role of visual objects such as memes in the spread of disinformation on WhatsApp has been an important point of discussion (Abidin, 2020; Evangelista & Bruno, 2019). Researchers have highlighted similar concerns about the role of audio messaging (El-Masri et al., 2022; Kischinhevsky et al., 2020; Maros et al., 2021). As discussed in chapter 3, audio messaging helps users maintain relationships with friends and family by affording tonal modulation and emotional expression, more difficult to convey via text. Research shows how the same features of audio messaging enable it to function as a vehicle for disinformation, with worrying implications for election and public health campaigns.

Following far-right candidate Jair Bolsonaro's election win in Brazil in 2018, considerable research was devoted to studying the role WhatsApp played in the result. Three studies focus specifically on the role audio-messaging played in propagating disinformation to manipulate public discourse (Kischinhevsky et al., 2020; Maros et al., 2021, Resende et al., 2019). All studies examine the qualities of audio messages that help to accelerate disinformation campaigns and also help to make them effective. Kischinhevsky et al. (2020) found that audio messages play an important role as a source of information 'for voters with limited media literacy and difficulty to fact check information' (p. 140). Audio analysis revealed that voice notes replicate radio communication techniques like 'colloquial speech, tactics of persuasion and intimacy with the listener' (p. 142). As a result, audio broadcasts are often regarded as a trusted, authoritative medium for news and information. Audio notes were found to have discredited the opposition; raised public anxiety about the legitimacy of the election outcome; stoked fears of 'eroticization' and 'indoctrination of children' as a result of tolerance towards LGBTIQ+ rights claims; and spread false information about opposition party proposals such as giving 'free rooms' to homeless people and drug addicts.

Resende et al. (2019) analysed large numbers of audios containing misinformation, and found that their linguistic structure mimicked some elements of chain mails. This included use of emotive language, common structural elements including calls for action and the portrayal of scapegoats (Resende et al., 2019). Maros et al. (2021) analysed audio messages obtained from public, politically oriented WhatsApp groups in Brazil. They also found distinct differences in the linguistic qualities of text messages and audio messages containing misinformation, suggesting that audio messages expand the repertoires for articulating misinformation. To persuade the public regarding the authenticity and legitimacy of the audio message, and to increase its likely propagation, audio notes tended to try to establish a connection with 'someone important' – a celebrity or authoritative figure, like a doctor – as a 'strategy to bring credibility to the information being transmitted' (Maros et al., 2022, p. 94). Similarly, El-Masri et al. (2022) found that WhatsApp voice notes played an important role in manipulating health-related information and spreading misinformation in Lebanon, but Pasquetto et al. (2022) found that audio messages were more effective than text messages in debunking misinformation.

Regulation

As noted in this and previous chapters, design changes introduced to WhatsApp after Meta's purchase have steadily transformed it from a private chatting app into a global communication platform. Processes of platformization in the technical dimension, as outlined in chapter 2, have transformed WhatsApp by allowing media organizations and other public and private entities to reach into WhatsApp to distribute news and other media content, while Broadcast lists have also enabled organizations to coordinate and distribute content at scale across private WhatsApp groups. Other design changes which allow strangers to come together in publicly searchable discussion groups have grown the capacity for social appropriation, participation and public formation, inviting users to engage in illegal and harmful activities that have produced 'information disorders'. WhatsApp has also become a platform for political campaigning and public address in some countries, with political parties seeking to exploit WhatsApp's embeddedness in the daily lives of users and its incredible reach, to manipulate election outcomes. These developments have become increasingly difficult for Meta to control, particularly after the introduction of encryption, which removes oversight and limits the ability to moderate content, and this places WhatsApp and Meta firmly in the crosshairs of governments and regulators.

Chapter 2 focused on the EU's response to data sharing and privacy policy changes introduced by Meta to increase interoperability and functionality for business end-users, which came at the cost of other users' privacy. In the EU, WhatsApp and Meta must comply with data and privacy protection laws, and many other regulators around the world are following suit to improve their own data protection frameworks. At the same time, use of WhatsApp's encrypted design to amplify and spread hateful content and misinformation has led to an opposing regulatory push for less privacy, as encryption-breaking laws have been introduced and/or debated in Australia, the US, India and the UK, to address the problem of 'bad actors' misusing the platform.

WhatsApp and Meta have been vocal regarding the harm that would come from regulating against encryption. Will

Cathcart, current CEO of WhatsApp, took the drastic action of suing the Indian government over new laws that compel tech companies to provide information regarding 'first originator of information' (Porter, 2021; see also Gursky & Woolley, 2021). Similar so-called 'traceability' laws have also been considered in Brazil (Rodriguez & Schoen, 2020), and the EU is currently debating controversial measures to mandate technological interoperability across rival technological systems to increase competition. In response, Cathcart expressed concern that the laws would require breaking encryption, while also compromising the platforms' ability to limit spam and misinformation (Newton, 2022). Of course, these measures would also significantly disrupt WhatsApp's commercial and business ambitions, which we discuss further in chapters 5 and 6. But concerns have also been expressed by researchers and privacy advocates that laws to break encryption would usher in a new era of mass surveillance, that would put human rights campaigners at risk and embolden authoritarian governments (Gursky & Woolley, 2021; Hintz et al., 2019).

So far, in response to pushes for more regulation, Meta has tightened its terms of use and community guidelines, and offered technical solutions that do not require changes to encryption. The most common response in the technical backend has been the strategy to limit the number of times a single piece of content can be forwarded to other groups (limit reduced to five) and the labelling of content that has been mass forwarded. The strategy, intended to introduce 'friction' into sharing practices on WhatsApp, was reinforced during COVID-19, with an announcement on 7 April 2020 that it would be limiting the amount of times content is shared to only 'one chat at a time'.[8] WhatsApp also moderates content if users report it via the in-built flagging mechanism. When users report other users, WhatsApp receives the last five messages the reported user or group sent to the person reporting that account. Reported users are not notified about having been reported, and WhatsApp employs reviewers to go through the content and determine whether to ban accounts they believe are in breach of their Terms of Service. Based on interviews with WhatsApp moderators, *ProPublica* reported that each reviewer 'handles upwards of 600' cases per day, which gives them 'less than a minute' per case (Elkind et al., 2021).

The problem, though, is that the users are aware that WhatsApp moderates content despite encryption and they use it as a tool to prank or silence other users. One of the moderators quoted in a *ProPublica* piece about how WhatsApp uses AI to proactively monitor non-encrypted information (e.g., group names) explained that in Brazil and Mexico, 'AI was banning groups left and right because people were messing with their friends by changing their group names' and then reporting them. 'At the worst of it, we were probably getting tens of thousands of those. They figured out some words the algorithm did not like', a moderator told *ProPublica*.

Content moderation on WhatsApp is another example of the tensions that arise from the platform's competing design choices: on the one hand, it has encryption and it still claims it promotes privacy by design and, on the other, it is moderating content and progressively investing efforts into transforming WhatsApp into a more 'public' communication platform via the constant increase of the number of people that can participate in groups, the possibility to share links to groups on the open web and the constant development of the WhatsApp Business API, which allows businesses to communicate with their customers at scale. We further explore this tension in chapter 5.

Conclusion

In this chapter we have illustrated how WhatsApp's capabilities for security, coordination, news-sharing and broadcasting have transformed it from a site for everyday, interpersonal communication into a global communication platform. By providing opportunities for civic participation, discussion of newsworthy topics among strangers and forms of public address, WhatsApp empowers group admins to enrol users into 'publics' leading it to resemble a 'town square' similar to other social media platforms. On the one hand, this fosters democratic expression and civic participation. On the other hand, it has provided opportunities for misuse, with actors spreading misinformation and hate, and contributing to 'information disorder' (Wardle & Derakhshan, 2017). We have engaged critically with these issues, exploring how WhatsApp has become a key focus of policy discussions concerning the role platforms play in democratic societies.

We have addressed these concerns by, first, looking at how WhatsApp's semi-closed architecture and encryption has enabled activists to safely communicate and organize in places where government surveillance, censorship and repression may otherwise limit these activities. We also considered how WhatsApp extends possibilities for activists to mobilize and coordinate volunteers by using WhatsApp's Group feature, multimodal affordances and admin controls.

Second, we considered the impact WhatsApp has had on news consumption and journalistic practices of communicating with the public. In response to global trends which have seen instant messaging platforms like WhatsApp become people's preferred site to share and discuss news, we explore how the introduction of media-sharing and broadcasting capabilities (media share buttons, Broadcast list features and WhatsApp's Forward function) have made WhatsApp the third largest gateway for news globally. We argue that these features have allowed media and news organizations to benefit from 'network effects', tapping into WhatsApp's large user base to directly distribute content and grow their audience. The Broadcast list feature has also led journalists to innovate new ways of engaging and informing audiences on WhatsApp by personalizing news. Conversely, WhatsApp's

Group invite feature allows news and discussion to take place in large, 'public' groups, where admins can publish links to groups on the open web (websites, blogs and social media pages), turning WhatsApp into a powerful tool for mass communication and persuasion.

Third, the chapter extended this focus to consider how WhatsApp's capabilities for easy sharing and its status as a 'safe space' for building networks of trust has been exploited by people to spread misinformation and other harmful information in the service of powerful political interests. We examined this by focusing on highly publicized election campaigns in India, Brazil and Nigeria, where political campaigners used what we describe as an 'information disorder' playbook to mobilize support and discredit opponents. This playbook involved practices of bulk and automated messaging; use of cybertroopers to surreptitiously manipulate public discourse; and exploitation of WhatsApp's multimodal features (text, video, photos, memes and audios) to spread false information and sow hate and division. The chapter interspersed these global examples of misuse with actions taken by Meta, including the reduction of the Forward limit in the wake of lynchings and deaths caused by rumour and misinformation in India, and opportunities to report harmful content.

But encryption remains an issue that has frustrated regulators and governments, limiting the ability for Meta to moderate content on the platform and restrict misuse. This has led to calls for greater regulation of WhatsApp in the form of 'traceability laws' and other regulatory measures to rein in forms of harm and abuse that threaten the democratic fabric of societies. These calls reinforce our argument that WhatsApp is much more than an app for private, interpersonal communication. Instead, as we argue throughout the book, WhatsApp has become a communication platform that hosts and enables the sharing of user-generated content among close contacts and strangers. It calls publics into being around the sharing of news and information, and allows political parties to mass communicate, coordinate and mobilize public support, often through methods that harm social systems. If platforms are defined by the necessity of moderating content to maintain public credibility and confidence (Gillespie, 2018), then WhatsApp fits this criteria, leading policymakers to push back on Meta's resistance to calls for more regulation. This will be further examined in the next chapter in relation to WhatsApp's platformization and growth in its economic dimension.

5
WhatsApp Business Model

On 17 November 2022, an entry titled 'Find, Message and Buy' was posted on the WhatsApp blog. The entry announced that WhatsApp was building a feature to enable users to search for and find businesses on WhatsApp's core mobile communication app, rather than having to leave the messaging service to do so. The feature allowed companies using the Business API – a WhatsApp product for businesses designed for large corporations such as airlines or banks – to be discoverable via WhatsApp's main communication app in key markets in Brazil, Colombia, Indonesia, Mexico and the UK. The blog entry also announced that WhatsApp was testing a feature that would enable users in Brazil to pay for products from within WhatsApp's main communication app, using their debit or credit cards. This mirrored an initiative that had been launched in partnership with India's premier online shopping platform, online grocery outlet JioMart,[1] several months earlier.

The announcement was a timely postscript to the job cuts across the tech industry that had dominated the news in the weeks before. On 9 November 2022, Mark Zuckerberg announced that 11,000 Meta workers would lose their jobs, a move that commentators linked to numerous ills including: the company's over-investment in the Metaverse technology, the general post-pandemic decline of online shopping (Murphy et al., 2022) and the decline of Facebook specifically (Sharples, 2022). On 17 November, following the previous day's gloomy outlook, Zuckerberg announced that business messaging on WhatsApp and Messenger would drive the company's future growth:

> We talk a lot about the very long-term opportunities like the metaverse, but the reality is that business messaging is probably going to be the next major pillar of our business as we work to monetize WhatsApp and Messenger more. (Dave & Paul, 2022)

WhatsApp's transformation into a business platform aligns with three strategic aspects for Meta outlined by Zuckerberg as early as 2012, well before WhatsApp's acquisition: 'mobile, platform, and monetization'.[2] In this chapter, we explore the interdependencies between the monetization of WhatsApp and its platformization, as well as how WhatsApp's evolution as a platform contributes to Meta's growth. By growth, we mean not only Meta's financial gains, but how the company is growing by technically developing its platforms in a way that allows it to create 'institutional partnerships and captur[e] markets' (Nieborg & Helmond, 2019, p. 200). This technical development of Meta's infrastructure, which involves interoperability among its various platforms (e.g., WhatsApp, Facebook, Messenger, Instagram), contributes to Meta's expansion in countries around the world.

WhatsApp's evolution as a platform for commercial exchange and business messaging addresses a question that has long puzzled observers since Meta's purchase of WhatsApp: how could the platform be developed to ensure return on investment? From 2018, WhatsApp started to tweak its design to cater to the needs of businesses and, by 2020, more than 50 million businesses were using WhatsApp to connect with customers via chat (see table 5.1). In what follows we focus on three WhatsApp business mobile products that contribute to its own platformization and to Meta's growth: paid messaging, click-to-WhatsApp ads, and WhatsApp Pay. We show how these features are scaffolded by a technical infrastructure that WhatsApp has been rolling out since 2018, including the Business App and the Business API, which are intimately interwoven with Meta's other APIs, apps and services. These technical developments, and the interconnected business models they enable, highlight WhatsApp's qualities as a multi-sided market, and its status as a platform. Below, we draw on key works examining the economic and 'transactional' dimensions of platforms (e.g., Athique, 2019; Nieborg & Helmond, 2019; Steinberg et al., 2022), to round out our argument that WhatsApp operates as a platform (not just a chat app).

WhatsApp's transformation into a business platform has not been without obstacles and pushback from regulatory authorities, states, competitors and ordinary users. In order to monetize, WhatsApp has technically evolved to satisfy those end-users that can pay to use the service: businesses. But this technical evolution is impacting the way everyday users experience WhatsApp's core communication app. In this chapter we draw on user testimony from India and Brazil, where many of the business-related features have been rolled out first, to show how WhatsApp's evolution into a business platform creates holes in the system, where the private data of users leaks out to predatory commercial operators, and where advertising messages flood into private users' accounts. This tension marks a key difference between WhatsApp and the Asian superapps it competes against such as WeChat, KakaoTalk and LINE. As explained in chapter 1, since their inception, superapps have had monetization

Table 5.1: Growth of WhatsApp business users and customers, in numbers

Date	Key Numbers
24 January 2019[3]	5 million WhatsApp business users
9 July 2020[4]	50 million WhatsApp business users. More than 40 million people view a business catalogue on WhatsApp each month
22 October 2020[5]	More than 175 million people every day message a WhatsApp Business account

Source: WhatsApp blog, Meta Newsroom. Table created by the authors.

in mind and have evolved according to this aim. Users of WeChat, LINE and KakaoTalk began to experience these superapps as marketplaces and digital wallets soon after they were launched. By contrast, WhatsApp started out as a private, peer-to-peer communication app that was explicitly marketed as ad- and gimmick-free. It is only in recent years that features facilitating commerce have been introduced into WhatsApp's official design and ordinary users are coming to terms with it.

This is not to say that WhatsApp's original focus on simplicity and privacy entirely precluded the scope for trade on the platform. From early on, business owners have appropriated features designed to facilitate everyday chat, such as groups, the in-chat hyperlink and photo features, to informally showcase products and secure orders, with transactions taking place in physical or virtual space outside of the chat interface (Nyanga et al., 2020). In their book on Twitter, Burgess and Baym discuss how the platform formalizes uses that arise organically, citing the Twitter hashtag, the @mention and the RT as examples. They refer to organically arising uses as 'appropriation', and the formalizing of these uses as 'incorporation'. WhatsApp's business features can be seen to traverse a route similar to the Twitter features described in Burgess and Baym's book, that is, from appropriation to incorporation: users 'appropriated' WhatsApp for business first, and then the platform leveraged this use and embedded it into its design through the Business App and API.

As it rolls out features designed to serve businesses, WhatsApp also faces pushback from regulators and central banks. Indeed, scholarship attending to the specific histories of capitalism shaping the superapp form alert us to the challenges facing the consolidation and global spread of WhatsApp as a business platform. Far from a blank canvas offering itself up for transformation (by WhatsApp), the places which are WhatsApp's largest markets, and those it is wanting to expand into, are already intricately woven 'tapestries' of markets, corporate institutions, and states and their policies. Steinberg et al. (2022) point out that much existing scholarship on political economies in an age of platforms presumes the state's potential as a benevolent regulator that is independent of platforms. But it is this presumption that overlooks the role states are playing outside of the US and EU as accelerators of the platform power of 'national champions' such as WeChat. While WeChat (and parent company Tencent) works closely with the Chinese government to expand and grow, WhatsApp (and Meta) need to satisfy (and contest) regulations in different countries to do the same. In particular, WhatsApp's plans to roll out its in-app payment feature, WhatsApp Pay, have involved protracted negotiations with central banks in India and Brazil. The platform is likely to face similar obstacles as it expands the feature to other countries, as we discuss below.

WhatsApp's quest for monetization

WhatsApp has long tried to find a balance between growing in order to monetize and remaining a privacy-focused messaging service. We may understand the development of WhatsApp Business features (chapter 2) as instances of building key affordances for commercial purposes on top of the core communication app that Koum and Acton built for 'simple, reliable' messaging. That is, the success of WhatsApp's monetization through its business features relies on the vast user base of its core messaging app, which has developed, through processes of social appropriation and technological iteration, into the largest user base of a messaging platform globally.

As outlined in chapter 1, when WhatsApp first launched it was available for a 99¢ annual fee, first on iPhone in 2009, then, in 2010, on Blackberry. When asked about the cost of the product, Koum and Acton published the following message for their user base:

> A small number of you have asked us why we don't switch to a free model and use advertising. The problem is that ads suck and ads suck even more on the small screen of a mobile device.[6]

Two years later, Koum and Acton doubled down on their promise that user experience would always come first, and ads would never be a part of WhatsApp, stating:

> We want WhatsApp to be the product that keeps you awake ... and that you reach for in the morning. No one jumps up from a nap and runs to see an advertisement.[7]

By 2013, WhatsApp announced that it would be free of charge for iPhone users and by 2016 – two years after Meta's acquisition – the paid subscription model had been completely abandoned. Part of the reason why Koum and Acton agreed to terms with Meta and sold their company in the first place was because of a promise made to Acton (see chapter 1) that Meta would freeze monetization plans for five years and that it would never introduce ads on the platform. Koum and Acton left WhatsApp in 2018 when it was evident that Meta was not going to fulfil its promise. At the time of writing this book, in 2023, ads have still not been introduced in WhatsApp's core messaging interface (Nieborg & Helmond, 2019), but Meta has been strategizing how to use WhatsApp to feed its ad business while bringing in other sources of revenue via its business solutions, as we explain next.

Paid messaging

Subscription models whereby users pay for using a service are part of WhatsApp's monetization strategy. They also play an important part in Meta's plans to diversify its revenue sources; Meta has launched similar models across its other services. In 2023, Meta launched 'Meta Verified', a paid subscription service for Instagram and Facebook users that targets content creators, allowing them access to specific features to increase the reach of their posts.[8] Since the 'creator economy'[9] is not as important on WhatsApp as it is on other Meta platforms, the subscription model on WhatsApp targets those actors that are willing to pay for special features, such as businesses that want to reach out and sell products to customers via chat. This is done through the WhatsApp Business API, which allows large companies such as airlines or hotel chains to message WhatsApp users at scale for a fee (chapter 2). As explained by Nieborg and Helmond in their study of Messenger (2019, p. 203), the introduction of paid subscription within Meta's 'family of apps' follows Zuckerberg's formula to expand into the mobile ecosystem: First, to develop 'ubiquitous utilities', such as messaging platforms, that billions of people in key markets would like to use or are already using. Second, to transform these 'ubiquitous utilities' into multi-sided markets by offering a set of APIs that provide third-party developers access to these utilities. Third, to roll out monetization on these utilities, for example by offering 'pro' features for those willing to pay for them.

In 2022, Meta signalled its strong commitment to keep developing WhatsApp business products because of their potential to drive the company's monetization in the future. 'The investments that we're making in product areas like ... the business messaging platform at WhatsApp are ones that we think will have a significant payoff for the ... business, both in terms of engagement and monetization', said Meta's Chief Strategy Officer Dave Wehner during Meta's third quarter 2022 results conference call. In fact, in the fourth quarter 2022 earnings report, Meta's family of apps 'other revenue'[10] (money coming from sources other than advertising) grew by 19 per cent, with 'strong business messaging revenue growth' coming from the WhatsApp Business API

(Meta Platforms, Inc., 2023). In early 2023, Mark Zuckerberg expressed enthusiasm for monetizing WhatsApp via paid messaging, with reference to its use by large airline carrier, Air France:

> Air France started using WhatsApp to share boarding passes and other flight information in 22 countries and in 4 languages. Businesses often tell us that more people open their messages and they get better results on WhatsApp than other channels. (Meta Platforms, Inc., 2023)

Paid messaging fees on WhatsApp vary according to geographic region (Constine 2018), and it is promoted as a service which enables various capabilities for businesses to drive 'marketing, sales and support outcomes' through chat, and to 'leverage the API to deliver compelling conversational flows' between big companies. This includes WhatsApp users and other intermediaries such as software companies.[11] Some of the examples featured on the WhatsApp Business blog[12] help to illustrate how paid messaging for Business API clients works. In one case study,[13] an Indian business was connected with a third-party business solution provider – a company using AI to provide customized messaging during high purchase periods (e.g., Diwali,[14] Black Friday sales). The AI tool was able to use data gathered from an individual customer's browsing and purchase history on the client's own company website to understand and respond to specific triggers (e.g., 'abandoned carts') with customized messages, sent via WhatsApp. Push-notification messages might also be sent to customers with product recommendations based on their browsing history. This demonstrates how paid messaging leverages WhatsApp's technical infrastructure – connecting business to developers to customers – in order to generate new sources of revenue through messaging that add more value than organic and informal exchanges between businesses and customers on the main communication app.

Feeding Meta's ad business

Paid messaging on WhatsApp is increasingly important in diversifying Meta's revenue sources, but WhatsApp also plays a vital role in Meta's main business: advertising. Nearly 50 per cent of Meta's advertising revenue derives from Canada and the US, but large WhatsApp user bases in Brazil, Mexico, India and Indonesia are also beginning to emerge as significant revenue sources for the company's advertising business. Officially, there are no ads on WhatsApp – even though Meta has attempted multiple times to introduce them via WhatsApp stories (the status feature).[15] Yet since 2018 Meta has found other ways to exploit WhatsApp's growing user base to feed its ad business. Meta has long relied on the harvesting of WhatsApp users' metadata to create personalized ads that target them on Facebook, and this is a business model that generates value from ordinary users of the core communication app as a 'commodity' that is sold on to Meta's paying advertisers. The launch of WhatsApp Business solutions in 2018 enhanced Meta's ad business, but in a slightly different way.

Both the Business App and the Business API allow and encourage businesses to buy 'click-to-WhatsApp' ads on Facebook and Instagram (in the News Feed, Stories and Facebook Marketplace). These ads contain a button that opens a chat thread on WhatsApp to allow businesses to communicate with customers directly. While the Business App is free to use and therefore does not generate revenue through subscription, it functions to drive up the value of Meta's other platforms as ad spaces, and therefore expands Meta's market of paying advertisers. 'Click to messaging' ads are an increasingly important source of revenue for Meta, representing $9 billion of the company's annual earnings based on quarterly financial performance data from 2022 (Meta Platforms, Inc., 2022b). Most of Meta's revenue from 'click to messaging' ads comes from Messenger, which can be explained by the fact Meta started to monetize this platform first. However, Meta announced in 2022 that 'click-to-WhatsApp' ads 'just passed a $1.5 billion run rate' which represents a growth of 'more than 80% year-over-year' (Meta Platforms, Inc., 2022b). The ad format 'click to messaging' is especially popular with small businesses in markets such as Brazil and Mexico, many of whom are new advertisers to Meta and want to advertise 'solely in this format' (Meta Platforms, Inc., 2022a). During the Q2 2022 Meta Earnings Call, former chief operating officer of Meta Platforms, Sheryl Sandberg, said that they were 'making it easier' for small businesses to create click-to-WhatsApp ads directly from the WhatsApp Business App, which would help these businesses 'find customers and grow' (Meta Platforms, Inc. 2022a).

Indeed, from the WhatsApp Business App interface it is very easy to buy 'click-to-WhatsApp' ads. Under the 'settings' section, the option to 'Advertise on Facebook' is the most prominent option. This option is also highly visible when a business tries another navigation path, such as clicking on the 'business tools' section within the app, where the option to advertise appears again (see figure 5.1).

So far we have discussed the business features of WhatsApp that serve to leverage the platform in its technical dimension to diversify Meta's revenue sources. First, the WhatsApp API, which is tailored for medium to large companies to communicate with their customer base at scale, enables paid messaging. Second, both the WhatsApp Business App and API serve to expand Meta's primary market of paying advertisers. A third feature, WhatsApp Pay, transforms WhatsApp into an integrated e-commerce, chat and digital payments platform. This presents another source of revenue generation for Meta and helps Zuckerberg's company to gain entry to the lucrative digital shopping and e-commerce space that has come to characterize emerging platform economies in Asia, as the next section examines.

Whatsapp Business Model

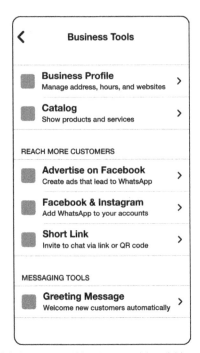

Figure 5.1: Artist's impression of 'Business Tools' available on WhatsApp for Business. In the 'Business Tools' section within the Business App, the option to advertise on Facebook and Instagram is prominent. Art provided by Phoebe Tan.

WhatsApp Pay

WhatsApp Pay enables customers to not only browse and select, but also to pay for items without ever having to leave the interface of WhatsApp's main communication app. When customers pay for items using WhatsApp Pay, Business Account users incur a 3.99 per cent fee.[16] It is unclear what proportion of this 3.99 per cent fee accrues to Meta (and what proportion accrues to participating banks), as financial statements of WhatsApp are not public. However, some business news journalists estimate WhatsApp Pay could result in $22 billion revenue for Meta over 'the next few years',[17] suggesting that the feature will significantly boost direct revenue in a manner similar to other digital payment systems, that is, through transaction fees.[18] WhatsApp Pay presents an interesting case for examining Meta's aim to grow in mobile-first markets such as Brazil, but also in some Asian countries where 'superapps' have reshaped platform economies by realizing the integration of mobile platforms, e-commerce and digital payments.

India is a good case study to understand Meta's growth ambitions and WhatsApp's platformization via its business features. WhatsApp Pay started testing in India in 2018 and was finally rolled out in 2020 for both peer-to-peer and business-to-customer transactions (Perez, 2018; Singh, 2020b). The feature uses a technology called Unified Payments Interface (UPI), a government-backed system linked to India's push to universalize digital payments and significantly reduce the circulation of cash in the economy. WhatsApp's entry into digital payments is the latest addition of a rapid transformation of India's e-commerce market. After the introduction of UPI in India in 2016, Google Pay and the Walmart-owned PhonePe entered aggressively into the digital payment space and, using gamification and cashback incentives to lure customers, soon superseded digital wallets. The main points of difference between UPI payment systems and digital wallets commonly found in superapps like WeChat are their relationship with banks and interoperability. In order to set up UPI payments, users need to have a bank account, whereas digital wallets can be loaded with vouchers or cash, and can easily be used by millions of unbanked people across the world, including in the Global South where so many WhatsApp users are located. Digital wallets such as Softbank, Alibaba-backed Paytm and Sequoia-backed MobiKwik, grew significantly in 2016 after the Indian government cancelled 86 per cent of the country's cash in circulation, but went into rapid decline after the introduction of UPI. With the rolling out of WhatsApp Pay, the digital payment sector in India is increasingly dominated by Big Tech and the banks that support the use of UPI (Christopher, 2020).

In India and Brazil, uptake of WhatsApp Pay has been facilitated by corporate mergers, acquisitions and alliances, which have allowed WhatsApp to insert itself into e-commerce spaces already crowded with local actors. For example, in April 2020, Meta acquired a 10 per cent share in India's Jio Platforms,[19] a multinational tech company that serves as a holding company for mobile telco operator Jio, as well as other digital services, including e-commerce. This move strongly resembles Meta's strategy for rolling out Free Basics in many countries in the Global South, as discussed in chapter 1. In both cases, Meta has struck deals with third parties that have allowed Meta to access an existing customer base. As both Goggin (2021) and Steinberg et al. (2022) argue, by acquiring a stake in Jio Platforms, Meta was able to leverage the former's dominance in India's e-commerce and digital shopping markets. Indeed, over the course of the next two years, regulatory body National Payments Corporation of India allowed WhatsApp Pay to be progressively rolled out to ever increasing numbers of WhatsApp's user base: first 20 million users (November 2020), then 40 million (November 2021) and then 100 million users (April 2022) (Chakravarty, 2021; Mishra, 2020; Reuters, 2022; Singh, 2022a). Shortly after the rollout of WhatsApp Pay to 100 million users, in August 2022, Meta announced the launch of its first end-to-end shopping experience in the country in partnership with online shopping platform JioMart, a subsidiary of Jio Platforms.[20]

This type of deal facilitates 'tie-ups' between local 'megacorps', like Reliance Industries, (Steinberg et al., 2022, p. 1410) and new entrants to the e-commerce sector, like WhatsApp, which can be key to determining the success of WhatsApp Pay. Local 'megacorps' have considerable influence with state actors and domestic finance firms and they leverage 'network effects' to create or lower barriers to entry to new players like WhatsApp

(Steinberg et al., 2022, p. 1412). In Brazil, for example, the rollout of WhatsApp Pay as a customer-to-business payment platform has been stymied by efforts to protect local players. WhatsApp launched both its peer-to-peer and customer-to-business payment services in Brazil in June 2020, but the country's central bank suspended the launch a week later over fears the service would compromise competition and user privacy (Paige, 2022; Singh, 2020c). In May 2021, almost a year later, Brazil approved peer-to-peer transactions, but not customer-to-business transactions (Pooler & Murphy, 2022). However, similar to the Indian experience, in Brazil, strategic alliances and partnerships have also helped to ease barriers to entry. For example, in December 2022, Reuters reported that Mercado Libre, the Latin American e-commerce platform, would be partnering with WhatsApp to allow customers to shop and pay for items in a WhatsApp chat, using WhatsApp Pay (Do Rosario, 2022).

The launch of WhatsApp Pay in India and Brazil is a significant step in WhatsApp's quest to become a major player in the lucrative e-commerce and digital shopping markets in Asia and Latin America. The progress with WhatsApp Pay's rollout in these places is good news for Meta, which is eager to diversify its revenue sources. But for ordinary users of WhatsApp's core communication app, there are downsides. In the next section, we explore the implications of WhatsApp's quest for monetization for everyday users, whose experiences of the platform are changing as WhatsApp increasingly prioritizes the needs of paying customers.

Business solutions – convenience or nuisance for everyday users?

In the opening of this chapter, we alluded to WhatsApp's November 2022 announcement that users would have the option to 'search' for businesses within the core communication app. With that announcement, the platform anticipated user privacy concerns by noting: 'We've built business search in a way that preserves people's privacy. What you search for is processed in a way that cannot be linked back to your account.' Meta's interest in monetizing WhatsApp via paid messaging, 'click-to-WhatsApp' ads and WhatsApp Pay is introducing new technical developments to WhatsApp's main chat app and WhatsApp's larger technical infrastructure, as we explained in chapter 2. For ordinary users, communicating with businesses takes place within the same app they use to socialize with family and friends. For those who are interested in using WhatsApp as an all-in-one app, the introduction of new business features within the core communication app might be convenient because they facilitate user–business interactions and economic transactions. But not all users are happy. In India, in particular, where the business features have been used for longer, news outlets have been warning about brands spamming WhatsApp users (Singh, 2022a), with some labelling WhatsApp as a 'spammers' paradise' (Christopher, 2022). In 2022, a study using survey data from 51,000 participants in 351 districts in India found that 95 per cent of respondents were receiving at least one promotional message every day. Of those, 41 per cent said they received 'four or more annoying messages on a daily basis'.[21] Most of these users (76 per cent) revealed they had experienced an increase in unsolicited messages and the majority (73 per cent) reported they were blocking the accounts responsible for sending them these commercial messages.

In Brazil, journalists were denouncing a similar trend. Blogger Gall DeBlasi, writing for the Brazilian *tecnoblog*[22] in late 2022, explained that although many of these spam cases were reported in India, Brazilians were also experiencing unsolicited messages from businesses. Other Brazilian outlets also reported a viral scam circulating on WhatsApp in 2022, which journalists attributed to changes in the WhatsApp Business API.[23] In India, too, journalists have attributed increasing spam on WhatsApp to the fact that it has become easier for businesses to register to use the API, and that an increasing number are doing so in order to push advertisements out on WhatsApp networks. Companies that used to build WhatsApp chatbots told *Rest of World* that, in 2022, companies sending out lots of spam were frequently banned, owing to a requirement that ordinary users had to check an opt-in box before companies could send them messages (Christopher, 2022). Later in 2020, however, the language surrounding the opt-in policy subtly changed; with businesses being *strongly recommended* to make opt-in methods user friendly rather than these being mandated.[24] This may have been a response to Indian users and developers who reported that businesses now rely increasingly on 'dark patterns' in order to initiate 'conversations' with users. In an article on the increase of WhatsApp spam since the concerted rollout of WhatsApp Business tools in India over the course of 2022, journalist Christopher conveys how he received a promotion message from an online travel aggregator which had obtained his number from a credit card payment app he had used to book a trip, which ostensibly gave the app permission to share his phone number with other services. 'This is a classic instance of a "dark pattern", where users are signed up to things they didn't mean to, and consumers find it difficult to discern how their data is being collected, stored, or processed', writes Christopher (2022).

Building on many smartphone users' familiarity with WhatsApp's main chat app, the Business App and API allow third parties to 'reach into' ordinary users' private conversational spaces, gather data about them and disseminate information that can be predatory in nature. This pattern has been especially noticeable in India, which has a large user base and where WhatsApp has been aggressively expanding its commercial arm. As a response to these reports of WhatsApp becoming a 'spammers' paradise', some European journalists have written[25] that a similar situation will not happen in the European Union due to the 2016 General Data Protection

Regulation (EU GDPR). In the EU, consumers are better protected from being sent unsolicited messages, by law, than other less regulated countries. Businesses are not allowed to send unwanted communications unless users opt in and they also have to offer customers easy methods to opt out of promotional messages. It is yet to be seen when and how some of WhatsApp's business features will be introduced in Europe. However, there are other important markets with less robust regulation regarding user data protection that might soon face similar problems to those reported in India. North America, for example, is WhatsApp's fastest growing region according to Meta's 2022 official documents,[26] and it could potentially be an attractive market to expand Meta's business messaging, and 'dark patterns'.

WhatsApp as a business platform

The development of WhatsApp's business model tells a story of its evolution as a multi-sided market (Gawer 2014; Nieborg & Helmond, 2019; Rieder & Sire, 2014; Rochet & Tirole, 2003), and supports our key argument that WhatsApp qualifies as a platform, not merely a chat app. In simple terms, as we have defined it in this book's introduction, a platform connects diverse end-users through complex digital infrastructures (Srnicek 2017, p. 24). Two years before the development of features tailored for business, WhatsApp had already conformed to this definition. As an intermediary responsible for harvesting WhatsApp users' metadata to feed the parent company's ad business, WhatsApp already enabled at least two groups to interact: ordinary users and paying advertisers. Before the launch of business solutions, WhatsApp also connected other diverse end-users such as news outlets and audiences via features such as Broadcast lists, as explained in chapter 4. As WhatsApp has begun to develop technical features designed to serve businesses, its platform infrastructure has become much more complex, and its interconnections with Meta have too, in a technological and financial sense. Meta refers to WhatsApp as a member of its 'family of apps' (Meta Platforms, Inc., 2022b), but WhatsApp itself is now a 'family' of apps in its own right, comprising two apps and a Business API, as well as different websites and extensions. Technologically and financially, these 'family members' connect with the parent company in a variety of ways, using various business models to reap profits from connections between 'heterogenous actors' (Plantin et al., 2018; Steinberg et al., 2022), including ordinary users of its main chat app, companies and third parties using its Business App and API, international banks, and advertisers using Meta's 'click-to-WhatsApp' ads. As a result, WhatsApp is struggling to satisfy all its end-users equally.

As Srnicek (2017) notes in his analysis of 'platform capitalism', 'since platforms have to attract a number of different groups, part of their business is fine-tuning the balance between what is paid, what is not paid, what is subsidized, and what is not subsidized' (p. 46). The story of WhatsApp's monetization offers an example of such fine-tuning. The platform is tweaking its design to satisfy the end-users that can pay to use its services – businesses – and this is negatively affecting the experience of ordinary users. Finding a balance is key for WhatsApp's success since it depends on its large user base to remain attractive to businesses wanting to reach out to customers 'glued' to WhatsApp. This is what we have been referring to in this book as 'network effects'. The more people use a platform such as WhatsApp, 'the more valuable that platform becomes to everyone else' (Srnicek, 2017, p. 45).

The development of WhatsApp as a business platform also tells a story of the diversification of Meta's revenue sources, which entails diversification of products and markets contingent on technological and industrial developments that enable new kinds of interconnections. Advertising has long been Meta's main source of revenue, but this is changing. The company's industrial development involves its advertising business but also other sources of revenue that could drive the company's growth, such as paid messaging and the addition of a 'transactional layer' (Athique, 2019) into WhatsApp via WhatsApp Pay. Meta's advertising business is constantly being plied and expanded with a combination of WhatsApp user data and new technological features for businesses to connect with customers through paid ads. But as well as selling advertising space, Meta is also in the business of selling bulk messaging capabilities to large corporations keen to leverage WhatsApp's large user base. In Srnicek's terms, platforms like Meta operate as both advertising platforms, 'which extract information on users, undertake a labour of analysis, and then use the products of that process to sell ad space' and cloud platforms, 'which own the hardware and software of digital dependent businesses and are renting them out as needed' (Srnicek, 2017, p. 26).

WhatsApp's transition to becoming a business platform, though, has not solely materialized through technological expansion and its interconnectedness with Meta's infrastructure. WhatsApp's increasing global reach as a business platform is only possible through strategic alliances and partnerships with local partners and megacorps to ease barriers of entry in key markets, as we have explained in relation to India and Brazil. This is a point of difference between WhatsApp and other, Asian superapps. WhatsApp shares with superapps infrastructural qualities such as 'embeddedness' in people's daily lives and 'extensibility' – meaning they are technologies on which a wide range of applications and extensions can be built (Plantin et al., 2018; Steinberg et al., 2022). But, unlike superapps, WhatsApp's monetization is complicated by its historical trajectory and the markets it wants to enter. First, WhatsApp was founded as an ad- and gimmick-free app, and introducing monetization contradicts this early vision that attracted many users to incorporate the technology in their daily routines. Second, while big players in the platform economies of Asia, such as WeChat, have the support of the state to become a 'national champion' (Steinberg et al., 2022), WhatsApp is a new player in many e-commerce markets, with well-established state–corporate relationships intertwined and strict regulatory contexts, and these are not always sympathetic to WhatsApp's ambitions.

Conclusion

In this chapter we conclude our conceptualization of WhatsApp as a platform, by exploring its economic dimension. We have explained WhatsApp's transformation from being mainly an unprofitable chat app that facilitated interactions between family and friends to becoming an increasingly profitable multi-sided market that facilitates interactions between diverse end-users (e.g., ordinary users, businesses, third-party software companies and banks). These interactions are enabled thanks to WhatsApp's technical architecture, which connects WhatsApp's main communication app and its users with small and big companies that use the WhatsApp Business App and the WhatsApp API. In its transition to becoming a business platform, WhatsApp is more than ever technically intertwined with the infrastructure that sustains Meta's 'family of apps' and this presents opportunities and challenges for WhatsApp's future.

The development of WhatsApp as a business platform clearly advances Meta's ambition to monetize WhatsApp and to diversify its sources of revenue. In this sense, it represents an opportunity for the company. As discussed above, an examination of the economic dimensions of WhatsApp sheds light on how Meta has found ways to make profit directly from the platform. First, the sale of 'click-to-message' ads on Facebook and Instagram helps to feed Meta's ad-fuelled business model. The popularity of these click-to-message ads in key 'mobile first' markets, such as India and Brazil, has led Meta to view WhatsApp as a key driver for Meta's growth.

Second, Meta is also diversifying its sources of revenue via paid messaging and WhatsApp Pay. Large companies pay a fee to use the Business API, and Meta gains a commission every time a user completes a transaction within the main communication app using WhatsApp Pay. These business solutions are key to WhatsApp's platformization. Companies pay to use the Business API because they want to reach out to the important user base that WhatsApp's main communication app has accrued over the years in many parts of the world. In this way, WhatsApp, like many other platforms, commodifies user data for profit – this user data then becomes a commodity to attract companies to pay for its business solutions.

The downside of WhatsApp's business solutions is that they are driving WhatsApp further and further away from Koum and Acton's original vision: that it would be a simple, privacy-focused messaging service that does not harvest user data. Despite business-to-user messaging on WhatsApp being encrypted, this does not limit the ability of the company to collect user metadata and transactional information. And the moment WhatsApp's user data becomes a commodity, user privacy cannot be guaranteed. Testimonies from India and Brazil demonstrate how, in countries where the WhatsApp business solutions have been rolled out for longer, ordinary users' disaffection with the service is on the rise. However, as we will return to in our final chapter, since WhatsApp is a key infrastructure for everyday life in some parts of the world – the 'switching costs' (Haucap & Heimeshoff, 2014) for many people to leave the platform are too high.

Finally, WhatsApp's platformization faces broader challenges. We have explained that while WhatsApp's main competitors in 'mobile first' markets such as Asian superapps have been in the game of e-commerce for longer, they also have benefited from supportive relationships with local governments and banks, or what Athique and Kumar call 'the licence of the state' (2022, p. 1420). By contrast, WhatsApp is a new e-commerce player, and its success in this industry depends on strategic alliances with local institutions and mega corporations in contexts where governments and regulators are not always willing to allow foreign actors to monopolize local markets, as the Brazilian case testifies. We further discuss these challenges in the final chapter.

6
WhatsApp Futures

In 2021, media scholar Taina Bucher published a book on Facebook in which she argues that there is not just one Facebook, but many (Bucher, 2021, p. 1). This echoes the sentiments shared by Nieborg and Helmond (2019), Burgess and Baym (2020) and other digital media scholars whose interest in examining how platforms evolve over time commonly lead them to centre their analysis on what seems like a simple question: what is [insert desired platform]? Invariably the answer to this question is much more complicated than the reader might anticipate. We have approached this book in a similar fashion. To borrow from Bucher's analysis of Facebook, there are many WhatsApps. WhatsApp is experienced very differently around the world in terms of how users have taken up certain features, and how this piece of technology has been adopted into the routines and habits of daily life. This is not only because users around the world have appropriated the platform in unique ways, but because WhatsApp has adapted its design to usage, while also addressing market friction and asserting its economic interests in slightly different ways in different markets.

In this book we have situated WhatsApp's evolution within a broader app and mobile ecosystem (chapter 1) and provided a broad overview of the platform's technological development in response to the needs of diverse stakeholders (chapter 2). From there, we have zoomed in on how WhatsApp affords intimacy among friends and family, as well as opportunities for self-expression (chapter 3), public communication and coordination among groups of people (chapter 4) and transactions between business, customers and other third parties (chapter 5). For most WhatsApp users, exchanges range from the highly intimate and private (such as sexting a partner) to the domestic (e.g., family group chats), the semi-public (e.g., neighbourhood groups), the public (e.g., engaging with political groups), and the transactional (e.g., paying for goods). This shows that, for ordinary users, WhatsApp is in fact a variegated communicative landscape and marketplace in which users alternate between, and also mix, different kinds of public, private and commercial address, and in which both strong and weak ties are secured and maintained.

Our key argument is that WhatsApp is more than a chat app; it is a platform. Like Nieborg and Helmond's (2019) work on Messenger, in this book we have analysed WhatsApp's technical and economic dimensions in tandem, while also considering a third dimension of WhatsApp's evolution: the social dimension. In this regard, we follow scholars that have called attention to the role users play in actively shaping platforms (Burgess & Baym, 2020; Gillespie, 2018) to show how users 'swarm' WhatsApp, appropriating it in ways that could not have been predicted by its designers and owners. The examples of user appropriation we discuss in the book are an important part of the story of WhatsApp's evolution, and of its platformization specifically. That is, studying the social dimensions of WhatsApp helps highlight how it functions to connect 'heterogeneous actors' or 'diverse sets of end users' (Plantin et al., 2018, Srnicek, 2017) – a defining feature of platforms. This challenges any view of it as a simple peer-to-peer chatting app. It also helps highlight how these diverse end-users (e.g., from ordinary users to journalists and businesses) have had direct influence in changing WhatsApp as a technology. Our analysis of WhatsApp's social dimension complements that of its technical and economic dimensions to provide a thorough and detailed account of its transformation, since its purchase by Meta in 2014, into a global *communication and business platform*.

The blueprint for WhatsApp's platformization, which Meta has tested on its other products (e.g., Bucher, 2021; Leaver et al., 2020; Vaidhyanathan, 2018), has applied the following formula: (1) growing the user base, (2) changing the design to cater to the competing interests of diverse end-users, especially businesses and, finally, (3) monetization. We have traced these steps from WhatsApp's very origins. First, when Meta bought WhatsApp in 2014 it was precisely because the technology already had a huge user base in mobile-first markets (Bucher, 2021; Goggin, 2021), where WhatsApp was outpacing Messenger as the preferred instant messaging platform. After the acquisition, Meta kept growing WhatsApp's user base, largely in the Global South, owing to business deals made with local telecom operators to make the messaging service free, known as Free Basics, which significantly reduced competition in mobile messaging markets. Free Basics attracted many first-time smartphone users to download and use the app, and this helped to shape its evolution.

Second, the technical dimensions of WhatsApp's platformization also need to be understood in the context of its quest to compete both with other Russian owned and US-based social media, and with the Asian 'superapps' (chapters 1 and 5), prompting changes in WhatsApp's design to include whimsical social features, and to enhance connectivity among a greater number of people via its Group function (chapter 2). WhatsApp's design has given rise to unique user cultures (chapters 3 and 4) – from WhatsApp-specific memes and other expressive content like stickers, to unexpected and lesser known uses of this technology such as public forums in Brazil, and the use of groups for political campaigning and disinformation. Some of these uses have driven unwanted attention towards Meta, as governments and regulators have called for more regulation to maintain confidence in media systems and democracy. Further, in its quest for differentiation among competitors, in 2016 WhatsApp rolled out a technical feature, encryption, that, somewhat disingenuously, posits its primary function as mediating 'secure' communication amongst peers. We have discussed how encryption satisfied end-users, such as pro-democracy activists, who cared about being shielded from government surveillance. But more importantly (for Meta's interests) encryption has provided a useful shield against repeated accusations that it does not care about user privacy, and to please users who shared Koum and Acton's vision of a technology free from ads, games and shopping.

We have also shown how WhatsApp has been developing new products and features to capitalize on demand for business communication via chat (chapters 2 and 5), digital payments and shopping (chapter 5). The business dimensions of WhatsApp are at odds with WhatsApp's self-presentation as a privacy-oriented and safe technology, although this is rarely acknowledged by its parent company. In part this is because Meta, after years of repeated scandals over its handling of user data, sees the value in using encryption strategically to avoid repeated calls for the platform to be subject to greater regulation and content moderation (Santos & Faure, 2018). The success of the strategy to date has led Meta to project the future of social media as shifting away from open networks towards private and encrypted services (Zuckerberg, 2019b). This vision, though, counters other changes Meta has made to WhatsApp's design in order to monetize the platform and grow as a company.

Monetization is the third step in Meta's blueprint for WhatsApp's platformization. Monetizing WhatsApp by selling ad space on the platform has proven difficult, because the founders' vision to keep the platform ad-free continues to align closely with user demand. Nevertheless, since 2018, Meta has found other ways to monetize WhatsApp: by selling 'click-to-WhatsApp' ads to companies seeking to attract new customers, and by charging businesses for the use of some of WhatsApp's services, such as the Business API, which allows large companies to provide customer service via chat at scale. In chapter 5, we showed how changes to WhatsApp in its backend – with the introduction of digital payments and e-commerce – signals an adaptation of WhatsApp's products to capitalize on new business user needs and consumer habits in mobile-first markets. This monetization strategy is a distinct move away from Koum and Acton's vision to keep the app simple, reliable and 'ad-free', with 'no gimmicks!'. WhatsApp's evolution into a business platform is opening a new era for WhatsApp, one in which the platform has become a 'pillar' of Meta's growth. This is reflected in recent revenue figures, which show that, while Meta's ad revenue has been declining, WhatsApp's projected economic growth and earnings counter this trend. This indicates that WhatsApp is a key piece of Meta's economic outlook until (or if) the metaverse experiment starts bearing fruit.

As a platform, WhatsApp has thus moved from a simple technical system to a complex one that now serves diverse purposes and satisfies different end-user needs via its multiple products: from the main WhatsApp communication app to its business services, APIs, and payment and web interfaces. The suggestion that there are many WhatsApps is not a metaphor. Depending on who you are, you could enter the platform from any one of multiple interfaces and apps that afford a different view, and enable different opportunities for communication, business and transactional exchanges. Depending on where you enter, you may be promised privacy and security, or be granted access to WhatsApp users' data and metrics drawn from the increasing interoperability between WhatsApp and Meta's larger infrastructure. In the remainder of the chapter, we consider the future of the platform, and also the lines of tension and contestation that have emerged – from ordinary users to governments to regulators – all of whom have called for a pause to Meta's ambitions for WhatsApp's monetization and growth. These tensions signal that platform growth has come at a cost to user privacy and trust in a platform once valued for its refusal to compromise user experience.

The 'next chapter' for Meta

As we have explored in chapters 1 and 5, the story of WhatsApp's evolution as a global platform unfolds in a context where US hegemony in the global communication market is unstable and constantly being challenged (Goggin, 2021, p. 57). It is also unfolding in a context in which Meta's own business and economic outlook is beginning to falter. According to a tally kept by *TechCrunch*, more than 160,000 tech workers were laid off in the first three months of 2023, which exceeds the total number of tech redundancies that occurred in the prior year (Mascarenhas & Stringer, 2023). The tech sector, including Meta, justified these layoffs with a need to cut operational costs and increase 'efficiency'[1] in the immediate years after the COVID-19 pandemic. But there are other reasons. For the first time in its history, in 2022, Meta faced declining revenue and made more than 20,000 employees redundant between 2022 and 2023 (Hern, 2023a). Meta's 2022 Q4 earnings showed a decline in advertising revenue across all its products and markets, with the company blaming these results on weak advertising demand and the emergence of TikTok as a strong rival in this space (Meta Platforms, Inc., 2023).

Meta knows that putting all its eggs in the advertising business basket has introduced vulnerability in its economic outlook and, in this context of uncertainty, has signalled that WhatsApp is the key to the company's diversification of its revenue sources. The role WhatsApp is playing in such diversification is especially pronounced in markets like India, Indonesia and Brazil, in which WhatsApp has a strong user base and which Meta sees as an avenue for growth. On 22 July 2022, Zuckerberg appeared live on American cable business TV channel CNBC and said that Meta's 'playbook' had been building services over time to 'scale the monetization' and that WhatsApp was 'really going to be the next chapter' for the company (Novet, 2022). Not the metaverse, but WhatsApp.

As chapter 5 illustrated, these new revenue streams arise as an outcome of Meta's desire (with its purchase of WhatsApp) to capitalize on a shift away from the dominant platform model developed in Silicon Valley, and to adapt to new platform economies, stakeholders and interdependencies emerging in mobile-first markets, particularly in Asia. As Goggin (2021) and Steinberg et al. (2020) claim, superapps have cleverly integrated e-commerce and mobile money with the simplicity and portability of mobile messaging, tapping into business and consumer needs in regions where 'communications and monetary transactions are entangled' (Steinberg et al., 2020, p. 1410). WhatsApp is aware of these shifting outlooks in global digital markets, which have also introduced interdependencies of tech companies with a range of corporate actors (e.g., banks, fintech and e-commerce companies, retailers) and state actors, who carry significant weight in picking winners and losers in the digital economy, and often champion local, or regional, players. As WhatsApp arrived late to the game (as outlined in chapter 1), the market conditions in some of its key markets have not always been favourable to it. We see this with challenges faced by WhatsApp in rolling out its digital payments feature in Brazil, and in the need to enter into strategic alliances to overcome obstacles to its expansion in regions seeking to contest 'data colonialism' (Goggin, 2021, p. 79).

While Meta's monetization and platformization strategy for WhatsApp has been adapted for mobile-first markets that represent the 'next phase in the [global] digital economy' (Goggin, 2021, p. 74), this evolution did not come about by accident. In 2012, Zuckerberg announced his desire to turn his company's core platforms and apps into mobile platforms and to work towards turning Meta's (then Facebook's) business 'into a mobile business'.[2] This vision, though facing challenge, has largely materialized, and is centred on WhatsApp as a player in emerging markets.

WhatsApp's development into a business platform has potential for Meta's commercial interests, and small and big companies are also benefiting from the platform's latest features. The WhatsApp business blog[3] showcases plenty of 'success stories' of entrepreneurs and brands around the world that are satisfied with the business solutions offered by WhatsApp. From a Turkish fashion brand that proudly states that the introduction of chatbots into its customer service has 'cut the costs of operating one of its call centres' to a snack food company in India that uses WhatsApp to allow customers to place orders.[4] Conversely, the business dimension of WhatsApp has introduced trade-offs, especially on the ordinary users' side of things. In chapter 5 we brought attention to testimonies from ordinary users of WhatsApp's core communication app in India and Brazil, who are experiencing the platform to be much spammier than before, due to the latest design changes geared towards commercial exchange. WhatsApp aims to roll out its business solutions globally, and more user backlash is expected. New developments in artificial intelligence chatbots such as OpenAI's technology, ChatGPT, offer advanced conversational capabilities that can easily be integrated into WhatsApp's business solutions, as explored in chapter 5, but whether these integrations are welcome or introduce further concerns around privacy remain to be seen. Since ChatGPT was released in November 2022, developers have written code and made it available on repositories like GitHub for integrating this AI chatbot with WhatsApp through the WhatsApp Business API (e.g., Soares, 2023). This increased interoperability, as we have argued in his book, will have deep implications for how WhatsApp is used and experienced around the world. We unpack these challenges in the next section.

Less simple, reliable and private

If we go 'back in time' to see how WhatsApp's website looked in 2014, when Meta bought the service, the platform presented itself as 'Simple. Personal. Real Time Messaging'

WhatsApp Futures

which could be downloaded and used across a range of mobile devices and smartphones (see figure 6.1). One could argue that this self-depiction was partially accurate. It was a simple app, yes, designed for and used exclusively on mobile phones at the time.[5] This facilitated its rapid uptake among diverse cohorts, including users in the Global South for whom desktop computers and broadband were less affordable than cheap smartphones and zero-rated data plans, as we explored in chapter 1. It was also largely personal, except in countries where everyday communication among strangers happened via large private and more public groups and in markets where the platform was already being used for businesses (e.g., Marasciulo, 2022; see also chapters 3 and 4). And it was real time. The concept of privacy was not even mentioned on the landing page, and the website menu tabs reinforced its simplicity: home, download, FAQ, Blog and Contact.

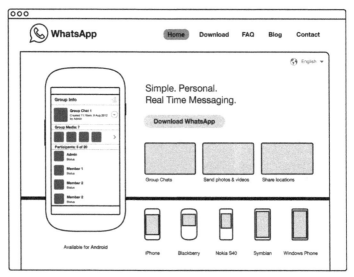

Figure 6.1: Artist's impression of WhatsApp's landing page in January 2014 based on website stored by the Web Archive (https://web.archive.org/web/20140102070018/https://www.whatsapp.com/). Art provided by Phoebe Tan.

Fast forward to 2023 and the website looks different, with business features having their own tab that, when clicked on, opens a new website, as explained in chapter 2 (figure 2.1). However, WhatsApp still presents itself to ordinary users in a very similar way to how it did back in 2014, as a 'simple, reliable, private messaging' service to stay connected with family and friends. We have argued that this self-presentation does not entirely hold true. WhatsApp's platformization makes the technology no longer *simple*. WhatsApp's latest redesigns, especially Communities and the platform's business solutions, make chatting on WhatsApp's core communication app spammier, and messier, and user dissatisfaction is on the rise in key markets such as India (see chapter 5).

To evaluate whether WhatsApp is *reliable*, one would have to ask its multiple end-users, including ordinary users, and surely answers would be neither consistent nor straightforward. Reliability is achieved when something or someone is trusted. But literature on trust in relation to technology or institutions shows us how difficult it is to fully trust a system (Pink, 2022). Expert in repairing stakeholder trust Nicole Gillespie showed this complexity using banks as an example: you trust them insofar as they will keep your money safe, but you probably do not trust they will protect your personal data.[6] In the case of WhatsApp, multiple outages show that the service is not always reliable and user data sharing with Meta is testimony to how the platform is also no longer *private*.

Similarly, as we have argued, encryption affords a level of *privacy* but this falls into the cracks when considering WhatsApp's other competing design choices, particularly since the development of its business integrations. WhatsApp is symbolically powerful in relation to Zuckerberg's 'privacy-focused' vision, despite the irony of this shift in priority after years of embracing the motto of 'making the world more open and connected'. As explained in chapter 4, WhatsApp was already used as a 'private' and secure platform by people in many parts of the world, especially activists, before encryption. This 'network effect' allowed Zuckerberg to use WhatsApp's reputation of trust among diverse cohorts to make encryption the cornerstone of Meta's future vision for social media. But while encryption affords private communication among pro-democracy actors and ordinary users, it also facilitates coordination among organizations and less credible actors, those who would choose to use this shield to hide nefarious and criminal activity, or to mislead the public and manipulate election outcomes. This, in combination with WhatsApp becoming increasingly a platform for 'public' communication and the sharing of news – thanks to its broadcasting and media-sharing capabilities – has put this technology in the spotlight for its links to misinformation and information disorder (Wardle & Derakhshan, 2017).

As a consequence, governments around the world are challenging some of WhatsApp's technical features, and we anticipate that this could impact this technology's credibility and future plans. For example, governments in Brazil and India want encrypted apps to provide 'traceability' – a method by which law enforcement could identify the sender of any message (Bansal, 2021). Recent debate about whether moderation of encrypted messaging platforms is a public good or a breach of user expectations and human rights has emerged as a key policy focus in work concerning regulation of platform infrastructures, with WhatsApp being a central focus of governments around the world. The increasing use of WhatsApp to perpetuate harm or misinformation has become a talking point owing to its wide availability and low barriers to use. This speaks to our conceptualization of WhatsApp as a platform in its social dimension in this book. It is not only an app that affords private communication among close friends, but it shares with other social media platforms the ability to converge 'content sharing, public communication, and interpersonal connection' (Burgess et al., 2017, p. 1). In this way, it has come to mediate public discourse, which, as Gillespie argues, not only helps to qualify it as a platform, but has also brought it under increasing pressure to moderate (Gillespie, 2018). And certainly these calls to moderate content circulating on the platform have intensified in recent years (Gillespie et al., 2020).

In 2018, Australian lawmakers were drawn into a tense debate between law enforcement and the tech industry as submissions were heard by the Parliamentary Joint Committee on Intelligence and Security, who were, at the time, debating a new Telecommunications Bill that would become known as the 'encryption bill' (McGarrity & Hardy, 2020, p. 169). The bill, which was passed into law in late 2018, compels tech companies to provide 'backdoor access' to encrypted communications on their services. In one submission, the Australian Department of Home Affairs claimed that 90 per cent of terrorism investigations are limited by encryption (p. 169) and that encryption-breaking laws were necessary to ensure public security. Tech companies including Meta, Apple, Google, Amazon and Mozilla objected to the law on the basis that undermining encryption could introduce 'systemic weaknesses' into communication technologies that could themselves be exploited by bad actors, and would undermine 'global consumer confidence' in privacy-enhancing technology (p. 170). Similar laws are being debated in the UK. The Online Safety Bill draft, which was reintroduced to the UK parliament in early 2023, grants powers to the UK regulator to require WhatsApp to implement content moderation policies that would be hard to comply with 'without removing end-to-end encryption' (Hern, 2023b).

Similar policy debates have arisen in the US, with US FBI Director James Comey arguing in 2015 that rather than passing laws that would force companies to comply with orders requesting backdoor access, communication devices and platforms should be accessible to law enforcement by design and 'through the front door' (Abelson et al., 2015, p. 71). While these debates were silenced temporarily by the Obama administration, which warned against encryption-busting bills, the Trump administration in 2020 passed the EARN IT Act under the guise of preventing the circulation of child exploitation material. Many critics, though, felt the bill encouraged 'the creation of backdoors by holding encrypted platforms accountable for illegal content' spread through their networks even if they could not access this content because of encryption (Gursky & Wooley, 2021, p. 3). This was followed by the EU, whose new rules to govern the use of encryption, drafted in 2020, used the rationale of needing to prevent paedophiles and terrorists using encrypted communications to pave the way for what privacy advocates consider likely future anti-encryption legislation.

On the other side of this growing sentiment for more surveillance and laws to break encrypted communications are privacy and encryption advocates, such as the Electronic Frontier Foundation. They argue that more regulatory approaches to encryption put citizens' and activists' safety and data rights at risk, while advancing scenarios where surveillance becomes unlimited, threatening democracies with authoritarian creep (Hintz et al., 2019).

These examples put WhatsApp and Meta's vision of encrypted platforms at the centre of global debates around content moderation, user privacy, security and freedom of expression. The future of WhatsApp as a 'private' service – and by extension Meta's plan to extend encryption to its other platforms – might be easily compromised in the next few years depending on how the emerging 'encryption laws' evolve around the world. Further, the idea of WhatsApp as a 'private' platform has been eroded from the moment WhatsApp invested heavily in becoming a business platform and merged its features with Meta's broader infrastructure. As a multi-sided market (Bucher, 2012; Gawer, 2014; Nieborg & Helmond, 2019; Rieder & Sire, 2014; Rochet & Tirole, 2003), WhatsApp is involved in a constant juggling act to satisfy diverse stakeholders with competing agendas and this also has deep implications for its future.

Spammier but still sticky

Transforming WhatsApp into a global communication and business platform has important implications for how ordinary users around the world are experiencing WhatsApp, now and into the future, particularly in key markets. As we have argued, while businesses access different WhatsApp services such as the Business App and API to reach out to customers, everyday users' experience on WhatsApp is centralized in one app (or two, if they use the desktop version to access the service). In parts of the world where WhatsApp is used as more than a chatting app, users have already reported that communication is becoming less simple and more messy and spammy, because brands are bombarding users with promotions and notifications without the platform offering robust controls to tackle this practice (Anwar, 2022; Christopher, 2022). Echoing previous issues related to the spread of misleading and problematic content on the platform, there are now problems regarding accountability for what is being sold through WhatsApp. In India users have complained about poor quality or misleading goods and services being sold by businesses via WhatsApp. Following a typical move by social media platforms, WhatsApp is neglecting responsibility by directing users to complain to the Indian Grievance Officer.[7] Under WhatsApp's Terms and Conditions, businesses are the ones responsible for resolving such complaints and must obey Indian laws for selling online. This growing user disaffection could potentially dampen Meta's growth in its largest market. Yet these issues around product safety and accountability are also seen in other big players in e-commerce, like Amazon,[8] and depending on how WhatsApp's business solutions expand in global markets, WhatsApp might face a similar scenario prompting the company to react to user, business and regulator complaints.

For the moment, though, this experience is limited to testing sites where the full array of business services has been rolled out by Meta. Moreover, there are limits to the speed with which WhatsApp can roll out the full array of business features across its key markets globally, as evident in the way regulators in both Brazil and India stalled the rollout of WhatsApp Pay. Additionally, the shift in the ways users are experiencing the platform may prompt them to switch to other platforms that afford the reliability, simplicity and privacy they prefer. Indeed, as discussed in chapter 2, changes to WhatsApp's Terms of Service and privacy policy in 2016 triggered user migrations to Signal and Telegram for those users who most valued the privacy affordances of WhatsApp. We wonder what these increasingly frustrated experiences in India, where WhatsApp has long been a 'do-everything' app, might mean for WhatsApp's current expansion and growth in US markets, where, as stated in chapter 1, messaging apps have hitherto been marketed and used as a more privacy-focused alternative to social media platforms. While encryption may provide some feelings of safety in these markets, a spammy user experience may limit its uptake.

Despite these uncertainties, as scholars have argued, in regions of the world where big players like WhatsApp enjoy market monopolization, the 'switching costs' (Haucap & Heimeshoff, 2014) for end-users are too high, making it difficult for them to leave the platform. This makes WhatsApp sticky despite a decrease in its quality or reliability. In a way, the outage described in the opening pages of the book provides some insights along these lines that are worth considering for the future of WhatsApp. This disruption to businesses and ordinary use for around 7 hours had a devastating impact in some countries, with business users reporting that the revenue lost in those hours could be, for them, the 'difference between paying the electricity bill or rent for the month' (Isaac & Frenkel, 2021). But the outage also demonstrated why many or most users in markets where WhatsApp is a 'technology of life' (Gómez Cruz & Harindranath, 2020) are unlikely to leave it to migrate to other apps or platforms, because the costs of doing so can be too high. This again illustrates the power imbalances between technologies such as WhatsApp and its users in some regions of the world, where WhatsApp's (and by extension Meta's) infrastructure *is* the internet.

WhatsApp as platform

Any study of a platform is a study of a complex, evolving technology (Bucher, 2021; Burgess & Baym, 2020; Nieborg & Helmond, 2019) where design changes and efforts to expand commercially are tested and responded to by an array of actors, including, perhaps most significantly, ordinary users. As already observed in relation to other platforms (e.g., Burgess & Baym, 2020; Gillespie, 2018; Leaver et al., 2020; Tiidenberg et al., 2021), users do not passively use WhatsApp as it was designed or intended to be used. Instead, they sit in judgement regarding every design change, resisting and negotiating them. Nonetheless, as we have illustrated in the pages of this book, many of these challenges are often blips in a steady narrative of increasing platform power and growth over time.

Platform scholars have alerted us to the reasons why the big corporate players (Meta, Apple, Amazon, Google) have grown to prominence and why, despite challenges, they continue to dominate global digital landscapes. By studying WhatsApp as a platform, we have considered how Meta's blueprint for platformization, pursued with Facebook (Bucher, 2021) and also Messenger (Nieborg & Helmond, 2019) has been adapted to markets and regulatory set-ups in mobile-first markets and in the Global South, where Meta has seen an opportunity. As noted in the introduction to this chapter, this blueprint, which has been so successful in growing WhatsApp into a global communication and business platform, has involved, first, growing users by offering an array of features that make experience of the service 'sticky', as examined in chapter

3. With this, users have created unique expressive content on the platform and developed diverse user practices that share qualities with other social media cultures regarding memetics, presentations of the self, connection and disconnection and the maintenance of close ties. The next step in WhatsApp's platformization has been the addition of business integrations and growing the connections between businesses and ordinary users, tapping into informal business economies that had already emerged in some regions such as Brazil and India where people have used WhatsApp for commercial exchanges and connections since its early beginnings. Monetization, the final step of WhatsApp's evolution to become a global communication and business platform, has seen WhatsApp rapidly merge with Meta's larger infrastructure. This has implications for end-users, for whom it has become clear that their data is being shared among these two companies and for whom their experience of socializing on WhatsApp will inevitably change. It also has implications for regulators trying to put a cap on Meta's expansion and ambition to become the 'operating system of our lives' (Vaidhyanathan, 2018) on a global scale.

Meta has fought and continues to fight to consolidate WhatsApp business solutions, such as the integration of WhatsApp Pay. As explored in chapter 5, while there are fewer limitations in markets that do not regulate competition so closely, in Western countries and Brazil, regulators are increasingly placing limits on Meta's (and WhatsApp's) growth (e.g., Paige, 2022; Pereira et al., 2022). Similarly, anti-trust cases against Meta in the US, EU and Turkey, owing to the convergence of data collected from Meta's increasingly integrated platforms – Instagram, Facebook and WhatsApp – show that Meta's efforts to consolidate and increase its platform power continues to face barriers and challenge. Notwithstanding the increasing powers that states and regulators have to disrupt platforms, so far the tale told of platforms is that, as major shapers of global platform economies, they also have a status of being too big to fail. It would be a brave response for regulators to completely chop off the head of a business whose tentacles reach deep into the life-worlds of so many people around the world, and for whom scaling back WhatsApp's growth may have consequences similar to the outage described in the Introduction, but on a much larger scale.

Conclusion

In charting some narrative arcs of WhatsApp's development into the future in this book, we acknowledge that the 'next chapter' is by no means certain. But we are confident that we will learn more about WhatsApp's future by studying it as a global communication and business platform that has implications for Meta's industrial development. As we have also made clear, we could have situated WhatsApp within the growing field of literature on superapps, but to do so would also lock us into focusing on a particular chapter of mobile messaging apps and their intersection with Asian platform economies in a particular historical moment, while ignoring WhatsApp's origins in the US and Meta's refinement of its platform model over the years. While WhatsApp's platformization story is unique on the one hand, it is also part of a larger story for Meta. This makes WhatsApp an important focus of platform studies, although it has hitherto been largely ignored in this field of scholarship.

By conceptualizing WhatsApp as a platform, we have also contributed to mobile media studies, providing a pathway beyond the experiences users have on the main WhatsApp communication app in different regions of the world (e.g., Hassan & Hitchen, 2022). Focusing on these experiences is important, but it misses the larger picture we have drawn out in this book. Our aim has been to write a useful book for those interested in understanding how people use WhatsApp in different parts of the world. WhatsApp is a technology for socializing and intimacy, a public broadcasting channel, a social network, a place to do business and organize work. It is a *sticky* platform serving the needs of many end-users and creating interdependencies among them. But we have also written this book with a reader in mind who is interested in interrogating WhatsApp's platform power, and how this power is experienced and contested by different stakeholders. In particular, we have provided a framework to study this transformation and better understand it through breaking down our analysis of WhatsApp as a platform in its technical, social and economic dimensions, and examining the entanglements between them. As avid users of WhatsApp, we feel the 'next chapter' is not necessarily referring to some distant future, but is being currently felt in our daily use of WhatsApp, where communication is increasingly less 'simple, reliable and private', and more like you are engaged in a game of Twister, with one foot in the bedroom, one in the living room, one hand in the marketplace and another in the town square. We hope that by outlining and examining these transformations, the book provides insight into what WhatsApp means to its broad range of end-users now, and what its future possibilities are as this once simple technology grows ever more complex.

Notes

INTRODUCTION

1 https://twitter.com/Twitter/status/1445078208190291973
2 In some cases, we conducted interviews ourselves (Amelia and Ariadna in Malaysia and Spain respectively). In others, we relied on collaborators (Fiona Suwana in Indonesia) and research assistants (Niki Cheong and Gabriel Pereira in Malaysia).
3 https://developers.facebook.com/docs/whatsapp/
4 https://businessonbot.com/
5 https://blog.whatsapp.com/two-billion-users-connecting-the-world-privately
6 In simple terms, Free Basics is a program which made WhatsApp available to users for free in countries where data plans were often too expensive for users to access these services.

CHAPTER 1: WHY WHATSAPP MATTERS

1 Report from Mobile Growth Association (2021) at: https://mobilegrowthassociation.com/how-whatsapp-took-over-latin-america/
2 https://about.fb.com/news/2022/08/shop-on-whatsapp-with-jiomart-in-india/
3 Zero-rating refers to the practice of bundling services and offering them for free, without network data usage charges being incurred.
4 Net neutrality refers to the principle that Internet Service Providers (ISPs) should treat all internet traffic and content as equal, a principle supported in law in many countries where ISPs cannot legally block, restrict or favour some content over others.
5 https://blog.whatsapp.com/facebook
6 https://blog.whatsapp.com/looking-ahead-for-whats-app
7 https://signalfoundation.org/

CHAPTER 2: PLATFORM BIOGRAPHY

1 https://www.fool.com/investing/2021/01/18/whats-going-on-with-whats-app/
2 @mention tweets are those tweets directed to someone by mentioning their account in the tweet.
3 https://blog.whatsapp.com/why-we-don-t-sell-ads#:~:text=We%20wanted%20to%20spend%20our,do%20every%20day%3A%20avoid%20ads
4 https://blog.whatsapp.com/group-chat
5 https://blog.whatsapp.com/reactions-2gb-file-sharing-512-groups
6 https://blog.whatsapp.com/new-features-for-groups
7 https://www.timeout.com/london/blog/top-five-worst-people-in-your-whatsapp-groups-012916
8 https://blog.whatsapp.com/new-features-for-group
9 https://blog.whatsapp.com/new-privacy-settings-for-groups
10 https://blog.whatsapp.com/communities-now-available
11 In this blogpost, WhatsApp stated that the platform worked with over 50 organizations in 15 countries to build Communities and that their plan is to continue building new features to enhance communication within and across groups.
12 https://blog.whatsapp.com/communities-now-available
13 In 2014, before Facebook's acquisition, WhatsApp presented itself as a service for "simple, personal, real time messaging". Available at: https://web.archive.org/web/20140102070018/https://www.whatsapp.com/
14 https://blog.whatsapp.com/why-we-don-t-sell-ads
15 https://blog.whatsapp.com/facebook
16 https://blog.whatsapp.com/setting-the-record-straight
17 https://web.archive.org/web/20141206023158/https://whispersystems.org/blog/whatsapp/
18 https://blog.whatsapp.com/end-to-end-encryption
19 The fact that WhatsApp was sharing group information with Meta was not disclosed in 2016's revised privacy policy but it was in 2021's update.
20 https://web.archive.org/web/20190618205325/https://www.whatsapp.com/safety/WA_StoppingAbuse_Whitepaper_020418_Update.pdf
21 https://www.whatsapp.com/legal/terms-of-service/revisions/20160825/?lang=en; https://www.whatsapp.com/legal/privacy-policy/revisions/20160825
22 https://blog.whatsapp.com/looking-ahead-for-whats-app

Notes to pp. 57–70

23 https://ec.europa.eu/commission/presscorner/detail/en/IP_17
   _1369
24 https://www.facebook.com/notes/2420600258234172/
25 https://web.archive.org/web/20221025123857/https://telegra.ph
   /Why-WhatsApp-Will-Never-Be-Secure-05-15
26 https://scontent-cph2-1.xx.fbcdn.net/v/t39.8562-6/328495424
   _498532869106467_756303412205949548_n.pdf?_nc_cat=104&
   ccb=1-7&_nc_sid=ad8a9d&_nc_ohc=IWPSrfRfNaUAX95wqKs&
   _nc_ht=scontent-cph2-1.xx&oh=00_AfBi9apowcU9QyKbMiIknh
   dtckxbnQRHSdPPFi8YdmoRMg&oe=645AE83C
27 https://faq.whatsapp.com/643144237275579/?cms_platform=
   android
28 https://faq.whatsapp.com/683043392411948/?locale=en_US
29 https://faq.whatsapp.com/3619539998129227/?locale=en_US
30 https://www.dataprotection.ie/en/news-media/press-releases
   /data-protection-commission-announces-decision-whatsapp
   -inquiry
31 https://www.whatsapp.com/
32 https://english.elpais.com/elpais/2012/07/09/inenglish
   /1341836473_977259.html
33 See, for example, news stories in the Sydney Morning Herald
   (https://www.smh.com.au/)
34 https://blog.whatsapp.com/more-changes-to-forwarding
35 https://blog.whatsapp.com/more-changes-to-forwarding
36 https://business.whatsapp.com/
37 https://blog.whatsapp.com/making-it-easier-for-businesses-of-all
   -sizes-to-get-started-on-whatsapp
38 https://blog.whatsapp.com/introducing-the-whats-app-business
   -app
39 https://blog.whatsapp.com/introducing-the-whats-app-business
   -app
40 https://blog.whatsapp.com/celebrating-one-year-of-whats-app
   -business-with-new-web-and-desktop-features
41 In May 2022, Zuckerberg announced plans to offer a 'premium'
   version of the Business App for a fee, which would allow
   businesses to manage chats across up to 10 devices (see also
   Perez, 2022).
42 https://faq.whatsapp.com/794517045178057.
43 To get their accounts verified, business have to sign up to
   the Business API and verify their account on Meta Business
   Manager. https://respond.io/blog/facebook-business-verification
   #toc-mobile-3

44 https://faq.whatsapp.com/
45 https://www.whatsapp.com/legal/business-terms-20230427
46 https://english.elpais.com/elpais/2015/02/16/inenglish/1424084620_570764.html
47 https://english.elpais.com/elpais/2012/07/09/inenglish/1341836473_977259.html

CHAPTER 3: EVERYDAY USES OF WHATSAPP

1 https://www.timeout.com/london/blog/top-five-worst-people-in-your-whatsapp-groups-012916
2 https://blog.whatsapp.com/making-voice-messages-better
3 https://blog.whatsapp.com/making-voice-messages-better
4 https://blog.whatsapp.com/introducing-stickers
5 https://blog.whatsapp.com/introducing-stickers

CHAPTER 4: WHATSAPP PUBLICS

1 This was enabled via laws, including the Communications and Multimedia Act 1998 and the colonial legacies embedded in the Sedition Act (in 2015, updated to cover online communication), the now-repealed Internal Security Act, and the Printing Presses and Publications Act (see Johns & Cheong, 2021, pp. 733–4).
2 https://www.whatsapp.com/legal/terms-of-service/?lang=en
3 https://faq.whatsapp.com/361005896189245
4 Although media can be shared from open platforms "in" to WhatsApp groups, WhatsApp does not allow users to forward content "outside" of its closed system.
5 Memetic media describes the sharing of media texts (images, videos, screenshots, audios) which are created in such a way to invite transformation through recombination, making them popular internet forms that spread quickly (Jarvis, 2014; Milner, 2016; Shifman, 2014).
6 https://www.niemanlab.org/2015/07/the-new-york-times-is-publishing-on-whatsapp-for-the-first-time-covering-pope-francis/
7 In defining what these problematic contents and behaviours describe, *misinformation* refers to practices where false or misleading content is shared unintentionally, while *disinformation* refers to content that is deliberately manipulated

or fabricated and shared with the intention to do harm or to deceive (see Wardle & Derakhshan, 2017).
8 https://blog.whatsapp.com/Keeping-WhatsApp-Personal-and-Private?lang=kk

CHAPTER 5: WHATSAPP BUSINESS MODEL

1 https://about.fb.com/news/2022/08/shop-on-whatsapp-with-jiomart-in-india/
2 https://vator.tv/news/2012-10-23-mark-zuckerberg-lays-out-facebooks-vision-and-strategy
3 https://blog.whatsapp.com/celebrating-one-year-of-whats-app-business-with-new-web-and-desktop-features
4 https://blog.whatsapp.com/new-ways-to-reach-a-business-on-whatsapp?lang=tl
5 https://blog.whatsapp.com/shopping-payments-and-customer-service-on-whatsapp
6 https://blog.whatsapp.com/breaking-the-radio-silence
7 https://blog.whatsapp.com/why-we-don-t-sell-ads
8 https://about.fb.com/news/2023/02/testing-meta-verified-to-help-creators/
9 https://about.fb.com/news/2022/11/exploring-the-potential-of-the-creator-economy/
10 Meta defines other revenues as: "net fees we receive from developers using our payments infrastructure and revenue from various other sources, within the Family of Apps segment." https://investor.fb.com/investor-news/press-release-details/2022/Meta-Provides-Additional-Details-on-New-Segment-Reporting/default.aspx
11 https://business.whatsapp.com/products/business-platform
12 https://business.whatsapp.com/blog
13 https://developers.facebook.com/success-stories/tata-cliq/
14 Diwali or the Festival of Lights is an important festival in Indian religions.
15 https://www.tnasuite.com/blog/ads-are-on-their-way-to-whatsapp /Whatsapp will start showing ads on status section VP Chris Daniels confirms. https://tech.hindustantimes.com/tech/news/whatsapp-will-start-showing-ads-on-status-section-vp-chris-daniels-confirms-story-81BpnAgerr3dvRJd1n4xwK.html
16 Although it can also be used for peer-to-peer transactions without incurring such a fee.

17 https://seekingalpha.com/article/4570223-meta-the-22b-whatsapp-opportunity
18 https://bfsi.economictimes.indiatimes.com/news/fintech/how-upi-business-makes-money-what-profit-margin-do-they-have/95985239
19 https://about.fb.com/news/2020/04/facebook-invests-in-jio/
20 https://about.fb.com/news/2022/08/shop-on-whatsapp-with-jiomart-in-india/
21 https://dazeinfo.com/2023/03/01/spam-on-whatsapp-is-on-the-rise-in-india-the-updated-privacy-policy-is-affecting-user-experience/
22 https://tecnoblog.net/noticias/2022/10/10/whatsapp-e-inundado-por-spam-ao-liberar-mais-recursos-para-empresas/
23 https://nucleo.jor.br/raiox/2022-05-19-whatsapp-abriu-as-portas-pro-spam/
24 https://developers.facebook.com/docs/whatsapp/overview/getting-opt-in
25 https://www.hello-charles.com/blog/whatsapp-spam-europe
26 https://s21.q4cdn.com/399680738/files/doc_financials/2022/q3/Meta-Q3-2022-Earnings-Call-Transcript.pdf

Chapter 6: WhatsApp Futures

1 https://www.facebook.com/story.php?story_fbid=pfbid0382g0bPjUPCEGVWwrJJvuNCEh0ZHgxT1q9mm3BMm9hMYKKqSxj2zaQaPeYBw3GFFel&id=4
2 https://seekingalpha.com/article/1978461-facebooks-ceo-discusses-q4-2013-results-earnings-call-transcript
3 https://business.whatsapp.com/blog
4 https://business.whatsapp.com/resources/success-stories
5 Prior to the addition of WhatsApp Web and the Desktop app
6 Example given in the ADM+S Symposium in Melbourne: https://podcasters.spotify.com/pod/show/adms-centre/episodes/2022-Symposium-Trust-in-ADM-e1n1mqe2
7 https://faq.whatsapp.com/698004984553506?helpref=faq_content
8 For example: https://www.miragenews.com/online-marketplaces-remove-thousands-of-954034/

References

Abelson, H., Anderson, R., Bellovin, S.M., et al. (2015). Keys under doormats: Mandating insecurity by requiring government access to all data and communications. *Journal of Cybersecurity*, 1(1), 69–79. https://doi.org/10.1093/cybsec/tyv009

Abidin, C. (2020, July 15). Meme Factory cultures and content pivoting in Singapore and Malaysia during COVID-19. *MisInformation Review.* https://misinforeview.hks.harvard.edu/article/meme-factory-cultures-and-content-pivoting-in-singapore-and-malaysia-during-covid-19/

Ahad, A.D. & Lim, S.M.A. (2014). Convenience or nuisance? The 'WhatsApp' dilemma. *Procedia – Social and Behavioral Sciences*, 155, 189–96. https://doi.org/10.1016/j.sbspro.2014.10.278

Al Zidjaly, N. (2014). WhatsApp Omani teachers: Social media and the question of social change. *Multimodal Communication*, 3(1), 107–30.

Al Zidjaly, N. (2022). Covid-19 WhatsApp sticker memes in Oman. *Discourse & Society*, 33(5), 690–716. https://doi.org/10.1177/09579265221120479

Alinejad, D. (2019). Careful co-presence: The transnational mediation of emotional intimacy. *Social Media + Society*, 5(2). https://doi.org/10.1177/2056305119854222

Athique, A. (2019). Digital transactions in Asia. In A. Athique & E. Baulch (eds), *Digital Transactions in Asia*. Routledge, pp. 1–22.

Athique, A. & Kumar, A. (2022). Platform ecosystems, market hierarchies and the megacorp: The case of Reliance Jio. *Media, Culture & Society*, 44(8), 1420–36. https://doi.org/10.1177/01634437221127798

Anwar, H. (2022, October 12). WhatsApp users are being spammed with countless texts from businesses worldwide. https://www.digitalinformationworld.com/2022/10/whatsapp-users-are-being-spammed-with.html

Babu, S. (2016, February 16). 037: WhatsApp business stories from India. FIR Podcast Network. https://www.firpodcastnetwork.com/037-whatsapp-business-from-india/

Bakare, A.S., Abdurrahaman, D.T. & Owusu, A. (2022). Forwarding of messages via WhatsApp: The mediating role of emotional evocativeness. *Howard Journal of Communications*, 33(3), 265–80. https://doi.org/10.1080/10646175.2021.1974611

Banaji, S., Bhat, R., Agarwal, A., Passanha, N. & Pravin, M.S. (2019). WhatsApp vigilantes: An exploration of citizen reception and circulation of WhatsApp misinformation linked to mob violence in India. London School of Economics and Political Science. http://www.lse.ac.uk/media-and-communications/assets/documents/research/projects/WhatsApp-Misinformation-Report.pdf

Bansal, V. (2021, May 27). WhatsApp's fight with India has global implications. *Wired*. https://www.wired.com/story/whatsapp-india-traceability-encryption/

Bansal, S. & Garimella, K. (2019). Fighting fake news: Decoding 'fact-free' world of WhatsApp. *Hindustan Times*. https://www.hindustantimes.com/india-news/decoding-fact-free-world-of-whatsapp/story-LQ79X96OOKrGo7MHuW3TMP.html

Bapaye, J. & Bapaye, H. (2021). Demographic factors influencing the impact of coronavirus-related misinformation on WhatsApp: Cross-sectional questionnaire study. *JMIR Public Health and Surveillance*, 7(1), e19858. https://publichealth.jmir.org/2021/1/e19858

Bashir-Badmus, K. (2018). Analysis of gender issues in selected WhatsApp status. MA Dissertation, Department of Linguistics, African and European Languages, Kwara State University, Malete.

Basu, M. (2020, March 3). Exclusive: How Singapore sends daily Whatsapp updates on coronavirus. *GovInsider*. https://govinsider.asia/intl-en/article/singapore-coronavirus-whatsapp-covid19-open-government-products-govtech

Baulch, E., Matamoros-Fernández, A. & Johns, A. (2020). Introduction: Ten years of WhatsApp: The role of chat apps in the formation and mobilization of online publics. *First Monday*, 25(1). https://doi.org/10.5210/fm.v25i12.10412

Baulch, E., Matamoros-Fernández, A. & Suwana, F. (2022). Memetic persuasion and WhatsAppification in Indonesia's 2019 presidential election. *New Media & Society*, 14614448221088274. https://doi.org/10.1177/14614448221088274

Baxter, J. (2018). Keep strong, remember everything you have learnt: Constructing support and solidarity through online interaction within a UK cancer support group. *Discourse & Society*, 29(4), 363–79. https://doi.org/10.1177/0957926518754414

BBC (2018, July 19). How WhatsApp helped turn an Indian village into a lynch mob. *BBC News*. https://www.bbc.com/news/world-asia-india-44856910

References

Boczek, K. & Koppers, L. (2020). What's new about Whatsapp for news? A mixed-method study on news outlets' strategies for using WhatsApp. *Digital Journalism*, 8(1), 126–44. https://doi.org/10.1080/21670811.2019.1692685

Bodle, R. (2011). Regimes of sharing. *Information, Communication & Society*, 14(3), 320–37. https://doi.org/10.1080/1369118X.2010.542825

boyd, d. (2010). Social network sites as networked publics: Affordances, dynamics, and implications. In Z. Papacharissi (ed.) *A Networked Self: Identity, Community, and Culture on Social Network Sites.* Routledge, pp. 39–58.

Broeker, F. (2021). 'We went from the anonymity of the internet into my private WhatsApp': Rituals of transition among dating app users in Berlin. *New Media & Society*, 146144482110292. https://doi.org/10.1177/14614448211029200

Brown, A. (2020, March 29). Government coronavirus apps and Whatsapp channel: Where to get them. *Canberra Times*. https://www.canberratimes.com.au/story/6702105/government-launches-coronavirus-apps-and-whatsapp-channel/

Brunton, F. (2018). WeChat: Messaging apps and new social currency transaction tools. In J.W. Morris & S. Murray (eds), *Appified: Culture in the Age of Apps.* University of Michigan Press, pp. 179–87.

Bucher, T. (2012). The friendship assemblage: Investigating programmed sociality on Facebook. *Television & New Media*, 14(6), 479–93.

Bucher, T. (2021). *Facebook.* Polity.

Burgess, J. & Baym, N. (2020). *Twitter: A Biography.* New York University Press.

Burgess, J., Marwick, A. & Poell, T. (eds) (2017). *The SAGE Handbook of Social Media.* Sage.

Business Help Centre (n.d.). About billing for your WhatsApp Business account. https://www.facebook.com/business/help/2225184664363779?id=2129163877102343

Caetano, J.A., de Oliveira, J.F., Lima, H.S., et al. (2018). Analyzing and characterizing political discussions in WhatsApp public groups. *ArXiv*, 10. http://arxiv.org/abs/1804.00397

Casaes, D. & Córdova, Y. (2019). Weaponised information in Brazil: digitising hate. Policy Brief No. 63. Toda Peace Institute. https://toda.org/assets/files/resources/policy-briefs/t-pb-63_casaes-and-cordova_weaponised-information-in-brazil.pdf

Chadwick, A., Vaccari, C. & O'Loughlin, B. (2018). Do tabloids poison the well of social media? Explaining democratically dysfunctional news sharing. *New Media & Society*, 20(11), 4255–74. https://doi.org/10.1177/1461444818769689

Chadwick, A., Vaccari, C. & Hall, N.-A. (2022). COVID vaccines and online personal messaging: The challenge of challenging everyday misinformation. Loughborough University. https://www.lboro.ac.uk/media/media/research/o3c/pdf/Chadwick-Vaccari-Hall-Covid-Vaccines-and-Online-Personal-Messaging-2022.pdf

Chagas, V. (2022). WhatsApp and digital astroturfing: A social network analysis of Brazilian political discussion groups of Bolsonaro's supporters. *International Journal of Communication*, 16, 2431–55.

Chakravarty, A. (2021, November 27). WhatsApp gets approval to offer payments service to 40 million users in India. *India Today*. https://www.indiatoday.in/technology/news/story/whatsapp-gets-approval-to-offer-payments-service-to-40-million-users-in-india-1881545-2021-11-27

Chawla, M. (2014, February 21). How will Facebook monetize WhatsApp? *Economic Times*. https://economictimes.indiatimes.com/news/international/business/how-will-facebook-monetize-whatsapp/articleshow/30793199.cms?from=mdr

Cheeseman, N., Fisher, J., Hassan, I. & Hitchen, J. (2020). Nigeria's WhatsApp politics. *Journal of Democracy*, 31(3), 145–59.

Chen, Y., Mao, Z. & Qiu, J.L. (2018) *Super-Sticky WeChat and Chinese Society*. Emerald Publishing.

Cheong, N. (2021). Disinformation as a response to the 'opposition playground' in Malaysia. In A. Singpeng & R. Tapsell (eds), *From Grassroots Activism to Disinformation: Social Media in South-East Asia*. ISEAS Publishing.

Choi, E. (2013). KakaoTalk, a mobile social platform pioneer. *Seri Quarterly*, 63–70.

Christopher, N. (2020, November 13). As WhatsApp Pay enters India, local fintech companies aren't happy. *Rest of World*. https://restofworld.org/2020/whatsapp-pay-enters-india/

Christopher, N. (2022, October 10). WhatsApp is now a spammers' paradise in India. *Rest of World*. https://restofworld.org/2022/india-whatsapp-spam/

Church, K. & de Oliveira, R. (2013). What's up with Whatsapp?: Comparing mobile instant messaging behaviors with traditional SMS. *Proceedings of the 15th International Conference on Human-Computer Interaction with Mobile Devices and Services*, 352–61. https://doi.org/10.1145/2493190.2493225

Constine, J. (2017, September 6). WhatsApp announces free business app, will charge big enterprises. *TechCrunch.* https://techcrunch.com/2017/09/05/whatsapp-business-app/

Constine, J. (2018, August 1). WhatsApp finally earns money by charging businesses for slow replies. *TechCrunch.* https://techcrunch.com/2018/08/01/whatsapp-business-api/

Cronje, J. & van Zyl, I. (2022). WhatsApp as a tool for Building a Learning Community. *Electronic Journal of E-Learning, 20*(3), 296–312. https://doi.org/10.34190/ejel.20.3.2286

Dahya, N., Dryden-Peterson, S., Douhaibi, D. & Arvisais, O. (2019). Social support networks, instant messaging, and gender equity in refugee education. *Information, Communication & Society, 22*(6), 774–90. https://doi.org/10.1080/1369118X.2019.1575447

data.ai (2022). Top-10-apps by all-time downloads, Worldwide, 2010–2019. https://www.data.ai/en/insights/market-data/a-look-back-at-the-top-apps-games-of-the-decade/

Dave, P. & Paul, K. (2022, November 18). Zuckerberg says WhatsApp business chat will drive sales sooner than metaverse. *Reuters.* https://www.reuters.com/technology/zuckerberg-says-whatsapp-business-chat-will-drive-sales-sooner-than-metaverse-2022-11-18/

Dechand, S., Naiakshina, A., Danilova, A. & Smith, M. (2019). In encryption we don't trust: The effect of end-to-end encryption to the masses on user perception. *2019 IEEE European Symposium on Security and Privacy (EuroS&P),* 401–15. https://doi.org/10.1109/EuroSP.2019.00037

Deutsch, A.L., Boyle, M.J. & Velasquez, V. (2022, March 29). WhatsApp: The best Meta purchase ever? *Investopedia.* https://www.investopedia.com/articles/investing/032515/whatsapp-best-facebook-purchase-ever.asp

Dixit, M. (2022, February 26). WhatsApp payments: Can it be a big game-changer in the evolution of payments? *The Economic Times.* https://economictimes.indiatimes.com/small-biz/money/whatsapp-payments-can-it-be-a-big-game-changer-in-the-evolution-of-payments/articleshow/89842316.cms

Do Rosario, J. (2022, December 8). MercadoLibre in talks with WhatsApp on business messaging payments – CFO. *Reuters.* https://www.reuters.com/technology/mercadolibre-talks-with-whatsapp-business-messaging-payments-cfo-2022-12-07/

Dodds, T. (2019). Reporting with WhatsApp: Mobile chat applications' impact on journalistic practices. *Digital Journalism, 7*(6), 725–45. https://doi.org/10.1080/21670811.2019.1592693

Dredge, S. (2014, April 14). WhatsApp now has 500m active users sharing 700m photos a day. *The Guardian.* https://www.theguardian

.com/technology/2014/apr/23/whatsapp-500m-active-users-facebook

Elkind, P., Gillum, J. & Silverman, C. (2021, September 7). How Facebook undermines privacy protections for its 2 billion WhatsApp users. *ProPublica*. https://www.propublica.org/article/how-facebook-undermines-privacy-protections-for-its-2-billion-whatsapp-users

El-Masri, A., Riedl, M.J. & Woolley, S. (2022, July 28). Audio misinformation on WhatsApp: A case study from Lebanon. *Harvard Kennedy School Misinformation Review*, 3(4).https://doi.org/10.37016/mr-2020-102

Evangelista, R. & Bruno, F. (2019). WhatsApp and political instability in Brazil: Targeted messages and political radicalisation. *Internet Policy Review*, 8(4), 1–23. https://doi.org/10.14763/2019.4.1434

Feldmann, A., Gasser, O., Lichtblau, F., et al. (2021). Implications of the Covid-19 pandemic on the internet traffic. In: *Broadband Coverage in Germany; 15th ITG-Symposium*. VDE, pp. 1–5.

Fernando, G. (2018, July 19). Social media trends: Why voice messages are replacing texting. *News.Com.Au*. https://www.news.com.au/technology/gadgets/mobile-phones/why-people-are-switching-from-texting-to-voice-messages/news-story/d36d6d8occoc71da168b4e8ec96924e7

Froio, N. (2021, October 20). When WhatsApp went down, Brazilian workers' jobs went with it. *The Verge*. https://www.theverge.com/22734705/facebook-whatsapp-outage-brazil-informal-workers-economy

Gajjala, R. & Verma, T. (2018). WhatsApp: Whatsappified diasporas and transnational circuits of affect and relationality. In J.W. Morris & S. Murray (eds), *Appified: Culture in the Age of Apps*. University of Michigan Press, pp. 205–15.

Gangneux J. (2021). Tactical agency? Young people's (dis)engagement with WhatsApp and Facebook Messenger. *Convergence*, 27(2), 458–71. https://doi.org/10.1177/1354856520918987

Garner, P. (2015, February 19). Facebook plans to monetize WhatsApp: Ads or mobile payments? *Market Realist*. https://marketrealist.com/2015/02/facebook-plans-monetize-whatsapp-ads-mobile-payments/

Gawer, A. (2014). Bridging differing perspectives on technological platforms: Toward an integrative framework. *Research Policy*, 43(7), 1239–49. https://doi.org/10.1016/j.respol.2014.03.006

Gerlitz, C. & Helmond, A. (2013). The like economy: Social buttons and the data-intensive web. *New Media & Society*, 15(8), 1348–65. https://doi.org/10.1177/1461444812472322

Gibbs, M., Meese, J., Arnold, M., Nansen, B. & Carter, M. (2015) #Funeral and Instagram: Death, social media, and platform vernacular. *Information, Communication & Society, 18*(3), 255–68. https://doi.org/10.1080/1369118X.2014.987152

Gil de Zúñiga, H., Ardèvol-Abreu, A. & Casero-Ripollés, A. (2021). WhatsApp political discussion, conventional participation and activism: Exploring direct, indirect and generational effects. *Information, Communication & Society, 24*(2), 201–18. https://doi.org/10.1080/1369118X.2019.1642933

Gillespie, T. (2017). Is 'platform' the right metaphor for the technology companies that dominate digital media? *Nieman Lab.* https://www.niemanlab.org/2017/08/is-platform-the-right-metaphor-for-the-technology-companies-that-dominate-digital-media/

Gillespie, T. (2018). *Custodians of the Internet: Platforms, Content Moderation, and the Hidden Decisions That Shape Social Media.* Yale University Press.

Gillespie, T., Aufderheide, P., Carmi, E., et al. (2020). Expanding the debate about content moderation: Scholarly research agendas for the coming policy debates. *Internet Policy Review, 9*(4), Article 4. https://doi.org/10.14763/2020.4.1512

Global Voices (2017). Free basics in real life: Six case studies on Facebook's internet 'on ramp' initiative from Africa, Asia and Latin America. https://advox.globalvoices.org/wp-content/uploads/2017/08/FreeBasicsinRealLife_FINALJuly27.pdf

Goggin, G. (2006). *Cell Phone Culture: Mobile Technology in Everyday Life.* Routledge.

Goggin, G. (2014). Facebook's mobile career. *New Media & Society, 16*(7). https://doi.org/10.1177/1461444814543996

Goggin, G. (2021). *Apps.* Polity.

Goggin, G. & Hjorth, L. (eds) (2008). *Mobile Technologies: From Telecommunications to Media.* Routledge. https://doi.org/10.4324/9780203884317

Goggin, G., Martin, F. & Dwyer, T. (2015). Locative news. *Journalism Studies, 16*(1), 41–59. https://doi.org/10.1080/1461670X.2014.890329

Goh, D., Ling, R., Huang, L. & Liew, D. (2019). News sharing as reciprocal exchanges in social cohesion maintenance. *Information, Communication & Society, 22*(8), 1128–44. https://doi.org/10.1080/1369118X.2017.1406973

Gómez Cruz, E. & Harindranath, R. (2020). WhatsApp as 'technology of life': Reframing research agendas. *First Monday, 25*(12). https://doi.org/10.5210/fm.v25i12.10405

Gursky, J. & Woolley, S. (2021). *Countering Disinformation and Protecting*

Democratic Communication on Encrypted Messaging Applications. Brookings Institution.

Gursky, J., Riedl, M.J., Joseff, K. & Woolley, S. (2022). Chat apps and cascade logic: A multi-platform perspective on India, Mexico, and the United States. *Social Media + Society*, 8(2), 1–11. https://doi.org/10.1177/20563051221094773

Hassan, I. & Hitchen, J. (2022). *WhatsApp and Everyday Life in West Africa: Beyond Fake News.* Bloomsbury Publishing.

Haucap, J. & Heimeshoff, U. (2014). Google, Facebook, Amazon, eBay: Is the Internet driving competition or market monopolization? *International Economics and Economic Policy*, 11(1), 49–61. https://doi.org/10.1007/s10368-013-0247-6

Hern, A. (2023a, March 14). Zuckerberg's Meta to lay off another 10,000 employees. *The Guardian.* https://www.theguardian.com/technology/2023/mar/14/mark-zuckerberg-meta-layoffs-hiring-freeze

Hern, A. (2023b, March 9). WhatsApp would not remove end-to-end encryption for UK law, says chief. *The Guardian.* https://www.theguardian.com/technology/2023/mar/09/whatsapp-end-to-end-encryption-online-safety-bill

Herrero-Diz, P., Conde-Jiménez, J. & Reyes de Cózar, S. (2020). Teens' motivations to spread fake news on WhatsApp. *Social Media + Society*, 6(3), 2056305120942879. https://doi.org/10.1177/2056305120942879

Highmore, B. (2002). *Everyday Life and Cultural Theory: An Introduction.* Routledge.

Hintz, A., Dencik, L. & Wahl-Jorgensen, K. (2019). *Digital Citizenship in a Datafied Society.* Polity.

Hjorth, L., Burgess, J. & Richardson, I. (2012). *Studying Mobile Media Cultural Technologies, Mobile Communication, and the iPhone.* Routledge.

Horwitz, J. (2015, January 29). Line reports 2014 revenues of $656M, reaches 181M monthly active users. https://www.techinasia.com/line-reports-2014-revenues-of-656m-reaches-181m-monthly-active-users

Iqbal, M. (2022, October 24). WhatsApp revenue and usage statistics (2022). *Business of Apps.* https://www.businessofapps.com/data/whatsapp-statistics/

Isaac, M. & Frenkel, S. (2021, October 4). Gone in minutes, out for hours: Outage shakes Facebook. *The New York Times.* https://www.nytimes.com/2021/10/04/technology/facebook-down.html

Jain, R. (2014, November 13). WhatsApp group chat invite limit

References

increased from 50 to 100. *Mobigyaan.com*. https://www.mobigyaan.com/whatsapp-group-chat-invite-limit-increased-50-100

Jarvis, J.L. (2014). Digital image politics: The networked rhetoric of Anonymous. *Global Discourse*, 4(2–3), 326–49. https://doi.org/10.1080/23269995.2014.923633

Jin, D.Y. & Yoon, K. (2016). Reimagining smartphones in a local mediascape: A cultural analysis of young KakaoTalk users in Korea. *Convergence*, 22(5), 510–23. https://doi.org/10.1177/1354856514560316

Johns, N.A. (2017). *The Age of Sharing*. Polity.

Johns, A. (2020). 'This will be the WhatsApp election': Crypto-publics and digital citizenship in Malaysia's GE14 election. *First Monday*. https://doi.org/10.5210/fm.v25i12.10381

Johns, A. & Cheong, N. (2019). Feeling the chill: Bersih 2.0, state censorship, and 'networked affect' on Malaysian social media 2012–2018. *Social Media + Society*, 5(2), 2056305118821801. https://doi.org/10.1177/2056305118821801

Johns, A. & Cheong, N. (2021). The affective pressures of WhatsApp: From safe spaces to conspiratorial publics. *Continuum*, 35(5), 732–46. https://doi.org/10.1080/10304312.2021.1983256

Kalogeropoulos, A. (2018). The rise of messaging apps for news. In N. Newman, R. Fletcher, C.T. Robertson, K. Eddy & R.K. Nielsen, *Reuters Digital News Report 2018*, Reuters Institute, pp. 51–3.

Kalogeropoulos, A. (2021). Who shares news on mobile messaging applications, why and in what ways? A cross-national analysis. *Mobile Media & Communication*, 9(2), 336–52. https://doi.org/10.1177/2050157920958442

Karapanos, E., Teixeira, P. & Gouveia, R. (2016). Need fulfillment and experiences on social media: A case on Facebook and WhatsApp. *Computers in Human Behavior*, 55, 888–97. https://doi.org/10.1016/j.chb.2015.10.015

Khazraee, E. & Losey, J. (2016). Evolving repertoires: Digital media use in contentious politics. *Communication and the Public*, 1(1), 39–55. https://doi.org/10.1177/2057047315625076

Kischinhevsky, M., Veria, I.M., Bastos Dos Santos, J.G, Chagas, V., Freitas, M. & Alde, A. (2020). WhatsApp audios and the remediation of radio: Disinformation in Brazilian 2018 presidential election. *Radio Journal: International Studies in Broadcast and Audio Media*, 18(2). https://doi.org/10.1386/rjao_00021_1

Kligler-Vilenchik, N. & Tenenboim, O. (2020). Sustained journalist–audience reciprocity in a meso news-space: The case of a journalistic WhatsApp group. *New Media & Society*, 22(2), 264–82. https://doi.org/10.1177/1461444819856917

Kresna, M. 2018. Hokky Situngkir: Soal Hoaks Pilpres 2019, 'Lebih Berbahaya Kini Pakai Cyber Army' [Hokky Situngkir on hoaxes in the 2019 Presidential Election campaign: 'Cyber armies are more dangerous [than bots]']. *Tirto.id*. https://tirto.id/soal-hoaks-pilpres-2019-lebih-berbahaya-kini-pakai-cyber-army-c4xH

Larkin, S. (2017, August 29). Facebook furthers WhatsApp monetization efforts with verified business pilot. *The Drum*. https://www.thedrum.com/news/2017/08/30/facebook-furthers-whatsapp-monetization-efforts-with-verified-business-pilot

Leaver, T., Highfield, T. & Abidin, C. (2020). *Instagram: Visual Social Media Cultures*. Polity.

Lee, A.Y.L. & Ting, K.W. (2015). Media and information praxis of young activists in the Umbrella Movement. *Chinese Journal of Communication*, 8(4), 376–92. https://doi.org/10.1080/17544750.2015.1086399

Lim, S. S. (2015). On stickers and communicative fluidity in social media. *Social Media + Society*, 1(1). https://doi.org/10.1177/2056305115578137

Ling, R. (2010). Texting as a life phase medium. *Journal of Computer-Mediated Communication*, 15(2), 277–92. https://doi.org/10.1111/j.1083-6101.2010.01520.x

Ling, R. & Lai, C.H. (2016). Microcoordination 2.0: Social coordination in the age of smartphones and messaging apps. *Journal of Communication*, 66, 834–56. https://doi.org/10.1111/jcom.12251

Ling, R., Fortunati, L., Goggin, G., et al. (2020). The smartphone decade: An introduction. In L. Rich, L. Fortunati, G. Goggin, et al. (eds), *Oxford Handbook of Mobile Communication and Society*. Oxford University Press, pp. 3–12.

Livingstone, T. (2014, March 23). After WhatsApp: An insider's view on what's next in messaging. *TechCrunch*. https://techcrunch.com/2014/03/22/after-whatsapp-an-insiders-view-on-whats-next-in-messaging/?guccounter=1

Lorenzon, L. (2021, December 9). The high cost of 'free' data: Zero rating and its impacts on disinformation in Brazil. *Data-pop Alliance* (blog). https://datapopalliance.org/the-high-cost-of-free-data-zero-rating-and-its-impacts-on-disinformation-in-brazil/

Loucaides, D. (2023, February 2). The Kremlin has entered your Telegram chat. *Wired*. https://www.wired.com/story/the-kremlin-has-entered-the-chat/

Lu, D. (2019, September 27). WhatsApp restrictions slow the spread of fake news – but don't stop it. *New Scientist*. https://www.newscientist.com/article/2217937-whatsapp-restrictions-slow-the-spread-of-fake-news-but-dont-stop-it/

Madianou, M. (2014). Smartphones as polymedia. *Journal of Computer-Mediated Communication*, 19(3), 667–80.

Maíz-Arévalo, C. (2021). Humour and self-presentation on WhatsApp profile status. In C. Xie, F. Yus & H. Haberland (eds), *Pragmatics & Beyond New Series, Vol. 318*. John Benjamins Publishing Co., pp. 175–205. https://doi.org/10.1075/pbns.318.06mai

Malik, A. (2022, June 18). WhatsApp now lets you hide your profile picture and 'Last seen' status from specific people. *TechCrunch*. https://techcrunch.com/2022/06/17/whatsapp-hide-profile-picture-last-seen-status/?guccounter=1

Manzhirova, V.S. (2018, June 1). Cómo hacer la broma Rajoy ha abandonado el grupo en WhatsApp. *tuexperto.com*. https://www.tuexperto.com/2018/06/01/la-broma-rajoy-ha-abandonado-grupo-whatsapp/

Marasciulo, M. (2022, August 25). WhatsApp grocery shopping is already huge. One startup wants to take it over. *Rest of World*. https://restofworld.org/2022/brazil-trela-whatsapp-grocery-shopping/

Mari, A. (2020, February 28). Most Brazilian consumers interact with brands through WhatsApp. *ZDNet*. https://www.zdnet.com/article/most-brazilian-consumers-interact-with-brands-through-whatsapp/

Maros, A., Almeida, J.M. & Vasconcelos, M. (2021). A study of misinformation in audio messages shared in WhatsApp groups. In J. Bright, A. Giachanou, V. Spaiser, F. Spezzano, A. George & A. Pavliuc (eds), *Disinformation in Open Online Media*. Springer International, pp. 85–100. https://doi.org/10.1007/978-3-030-87031-7

Martinez, M. (2018, December 11). Burned to death because of a rumour on Whatsapp. *BBC News*. https://www.bbc.com/news/world-latin-america-46145986

Marwick, A.E. & boyd, d. (2011). I tweet honestly, I tweet passionately: Twitter users, context collapse, and the imagined audience. *New Media & Society*, 13(1), 114–33. https://doi.org/10.1177/1461444810365313

Mascarenhas, N. & Stringer, A. (2023, April 13). A comprehensive list of 2023 tech layoffs. *TechCrunch*. https://techcrunch.com/2023/04/13/tech-industry-layoffs/

Matamoros-Fernández, A. (2020). 'El Negro de WhatsApp' meme, digital blackface, and racism on social media. *First Monday*, 25(1). https://doi.org/10.5210/fm.v25i1.10420

Matamoros-Fernández, A., Johns, A. & Baulch, E. (2019, March 13). Becoming more like WhatsApp won't solve Facebook's woes – here's why. *The Conversation.* http://theconversation.com/becoming-more-like-whatsapp-wont-solve-facebooks-woes-heres-why-113368

Matassi, M., Boczkowski, P.J. & Mitchelstein, E. (2019). Domesticating WhatsApp: Family, friends, work, and study in everyday communication. *New Media & Society, 21*(10), 2183–200. https://doi.org/10.1177/1461444819841890

Mbote, K. (2014, March 19). Kenya: Whatsapp, Twitter to remain big players in Kenya's social media space. *CIO Africa.* https://allafrica.com/stories/201403191263.html

McGarrity, N. & Hardy, K. (2020). Digital surveillance and access to encrypted communications in Australia. *Common Law World Review, 49*(3–4), 160–81. https://doi.org/10.1177/1473779520902478

McMillan, R. (2014, February 20). You may not use WhatsApp, but the rest of the world sure does. *Wired.* https://www.wired.com/2014/02/whatsapp-rules-rest-world/

Mehta, I. (September 8, 2022). Twitter is testing a 'share to WhatsApp' button in India. *TechCrunch.* https://techcrunch.com/2022/09/08/twitter-is-testing-a-share-to-whatsapp-button-in-india/

Mehta, J. (2015, February 4). How WhatsApp is changing the way businesses work. https://yourstory.com/2015/02/whatsapp-businesses-work

Meta Platforms, Inc. (2017). *Facebook (FB) Q2 2017 Results – Earnings Call Transcript.* Meta. https://seekingalpha.com/article/4091008-facebook-fb-q2-2017-results-earnings-call-transcript?part=single

Meta Platforms, Inc. (2022a). *Second Quarter 2022 Results Conference Call.* Meta. https://s21.q4cdn.com/399680738/files/doc_financials/2022/q2/Meta-Q2-2022-Earnings-Call-Transcript.pdf

Meta Platforms, Inc. (2022b). *Third Quarter 2022 Results Conference Call.* Meta. https://s21.q4cdn.com/399680738/files/doc_financials/2022/q3/Meta-Q3-2022-Earnings-Call-Transcript.pdf

Meta Platforms, Inc. (2023). Fourth quarter 2022 results conference call. Meta. https://s21.q4cdn.com/399680738/files/doc_financials/2022/q4/META-Q4-2022-Earnings-Call-Transcript.pdf

Milan, S. & Barbosa, S. (2020). Enter the WhatsApper: Reinventing digital activism at the time of chat apps. *First Monday.* https://doi.org/10.5210/fm.v25i12.10414

Milner, R.M. (2016). *The World Made Meme.* MIT Press.

Mishra, D. (2020, November 6). WhatsApp Pay finally gets nod to launch with 20 million users. *The Times of India.* http://timesofindia.indiatimes.com/articleshow/79071913.cms?utm_source=contentofinterest&utm_medium=text&utm_campaign=cppst

References

Morris, J.W. & Murray, S. (2018). *Appified: Culture in the Age of Apps.* University of Michigan Press.

Munk, C.W. (2022, August 7). Why Mark Zuckerberg is talking so much about Meta's Whatsapp for business. *CNBC.* https://www.cnbc.com/2022/08/07/why-meta-and-mark-zuckerberg-are-betting-big-on-whatsapp-for-business-.html

Murphy, H., Johnston, I. & Criddle, C. (2022, November 10). Meta job cuts provide a post-pandemic reality check: 'The bubble has burst'. *Financial Times.* https://www.ft.com/content/c73e861f-0d98-4b34-b5b7-25f7bc2e5d2b

Newman, N., Levy, D. & Nielsen, R.K. (2015). *Reuters Institute Digital News Report 2015.* Reuters Institute. https://reutersinstitute.politics.ox.ac.uk/our-research/digital-news-report-2015-0

Newman, N., Fletcher, R., Robertson, C.T., Eddy, K. & Nielsen, R.K. (2018). *Reuters Digital News Report 2018.* Reuters Institute. https://reutersinstitute.politics.ox.ac.uk/sites/default/files/digital-news-report-2018.pdf

Newman, N., Fletcher, R., Kalogeropoulos, A., & Nielsen, R.K. (2019). *Reuters Institute Digital News Report 2019.* Reuters Institute and University of Oxford. https://reutersinstitute.politics.ox.ac.uk/sites/default/files/2019-06/DNR_2019_FINAL_0.pdf

Newton, C. (2022, March 30). Three ways the European Union might ruin WhatsApp. *The Verge.* https://www.theverge.com/23001152/whatsapp-eu-digital-markets-act-messaging-interoperable

Nieborg, D.B. & Helmond, A. (2019). The political economy of Facebook's platformization in the mobile ecosystem: Facebook Messenger as a platform instance. *Media, Culture & Society, 41*(2), 196–218. https://doi.org/10.1177/0163443718818384

Nizaruddin, F. (2021). Role of public WhatsApp groups within the Hindutva ecosystem of hate and narratives of 'CoronaJihad'. *International Journal of Communication, 15,* 1102–19.

Nothias, T. (2020). Access granted: Facebook's free basics in Africa. *Media, Culture & Society, 42*(3), 329–48. https://doi.org/10.1177/0163443719890530

Novet, J. (2022, June 22). Mark Zuckerberg envisions a billion people in the metaverse spending hundreds of dollars each. *CNBC.* https://www.cnbc.com/2022/06/22/mark-zuckerberg-envisions-1-billion-people-in-the-metaverse.html

Nyanga, T., Zirima, H. & Mashavira, N. (2020). Withering COVID-19 storm: Survival strategies employed by informal workers in Masvingo Urban, Zimbabwe. *Management Dynamics, 20*(1). https://doi.org/10.57198/2583-4932.1012

O'Flaherty, K. (2021, 24 January). Is it time to leave WhatsApp – and is Signal the answer? *The Guardian*. https://www.theguardian.com/technology/2021/jan/24/is-it-time-to-leave-whatsapp-and-is-signal-the-answer

Ohashi, K., Kato, F. & Hjorth, L. (2017). Digital genealogies: Understanding social mobile media LINE in the role of Japanese families. *Social Media + Society*, 3(2). https://doi.org/10.1177/2056305117703815

Olson, P. (2014, October 6). Facebook closes $19 billion WhatsApp deal. *Forbes*. https://www.forbes.com/sites/parmyolson/2014/10/06/facebook-closes-19-billion-whatsapp-deal/?sh=4d52e0575c66

Olson, P. (2018, September 26). Exclusive: WhatsApp co-founder Brian Acton gives the inside story on #DeleteFacebook and why he left $850 million behind. *Forbes*. https://www.forbes.com/sites/parmyolson/2018/09/26/exclusive-whatsapp-cofounder-brian-acton-gives-the-inside-story-on-deletefacebook-and-why-he-left-850-million-behind/?sh=29803a103f20

Paige, W. (2022, April 21). Meta's grand plans for WhatsApp business payments in Brazil have stalled. *Business Insider*. https://www.businessinsider.com/meta-faces-problems-with-whatsapp-payments-in-brazil-2022-4

Pang, N. & Woo, Y.T. (2020). What about WhatsApp? A systematic review of WhatsApp and its role in civic and political engagement. *First Monday*. https://doi.org/10.5210/fm.v25i12.10417

Pasquetto, I.V., Jahani, E., Atreja, S. & Baum, M. (2022). Social debunking of misinformation on WhatsApp: The case for strong and in-group ties. *Proceedings of the ACM on Human–Computer Interaction, Volume 6*. https://doi.org/10.1145/3512964

Pereira, G. & Bojczuk, I. (2018, November 8). Zap Zap, who's there? WhatsApp and the spread of fake news during the 2018 elections in Brazil. https://www.gabrielpereira.net/posts/whatsapp-mit/

Pereira, G., Bueno Bojczuk Camargo, I. & Parks, L. (2022). WhatsApp disruptions in Brazil: A content analysis of user and news media responses, 2015–2018. *Global Media and Communication*, 18(1), 113–48. https://doi.org/10.1177/17427665211038530

Perez, S. (2018, February 8). WhatsApp has launched person-to-person payments into beta in India. *TechCrunch*. https://techcrunch.com/2018/02/08/whatsapp-has-launched-person-to-person-payments-into-beta-in-india/

Perez, S. (2022, May 19). WhatsApp ramps up revenue with global launch of Cloud API and soon, a paid tier for its Business App. *TechCrunch*. https://techcrunch.com/2022/05/19/whatsapp-ramps

-up-revenue-with-global-launch-of-cloud-api-and-soon-a-paid-tier
-for-its-business-app/
Pierce, D. (2018, July 8). Phone calls are dead. Voice chat is the future. *The Wall Street Journal.* https://www.wsj.com/articles/phone-calls-are-dead-voice-chat-is-the-future-1531051200
Pink, S. (2022). Trust, ethics and automation. In M. Berg, D. Lupton, M. Ruckenstein & S. Perez (eds), *Everyday Automation: Experiencing and Anticipating Emerging Technologies.* Routledge. https://doi.org/10.4324/9781003170884
Plantin, J.C., Lagoze, C., Edwards, P.N. & Sandvig, C. (2018). Infrastructure studies meet platform studies in the age of Google and Facebook. *New Media & Society, 20*(1), 293–310. https://doi.org/10.1177/1461444816661553
Pooler, M. & Murphy, H. (2022, April 19). Meta suffers setback with WhatsApp business payments in Brazil. *The Financial Times.* https://www.ft.com/content/6d32bd6e-9278-4eba-a64c-482492520ee0
Porter, J. (2021, May 26). WhatsApp sues Indian government over new rules it says breaks encryption. *The Verge.* https://www.theverge.com/2021/5/26/22454381/whatsapp-indian-government-traceability-lawsuit-break-encryption-privacy
Rababah, L. (2020). Speech act analysis of Whatsapp statuses used by Jordanians. *Review of European Studies, 12*(2), 28–32. https://doi.org/10.5539/res.v12n2p28
Rajput, R., Saha, A., Kumari, S., et al. (2018, July 15). Murderous mob – 9 states, 27 killings, one year: And a pattern to the lynchings. *The Indian Express.* https://indianexpress.com/article/india/murderous-mob-lynching-incidents-in-india-dhule-whatsapp-rumour-5247741/
Rall, S. (2022) You can now renew your vehicle licence via WhatsApp. Here's how. *IOL.* https://www.iol.co.za/news/south-africa/kwazulu-natal/you-can-now-renew-your-vehicle-licence-via-whatsapp-heres-how-e11e9598-6fdf-4f64-af4b-50a4a9b55d8c
Reid, A. (2014, April 4). BBC using WhatsApp and WeChat at Indian elections. *Journalism.co.uk.* https://www.journalism.co.uk/news/bbc-using-whatsapp-and-wechat-at-indian-elections/s2/a556343/
Resende, G., Melo, P., Reis, J.C.S., Vasconcelos, M., Almeida, J.M. & Benevenuto, F. (2019). Analyzing textual (mis)information shared in WhatsApp groups. In *Proceedings of the 10th ACM Conference on Web Science (WebSci '19).* Association for Computing Machinery, 225–34. https://doi.org/10.1145/3292522.3326029
Rettberg, J.W (2018). Snapchat. In J.W. Morris & S. Murray (eds), *Appified: Culture in the Age of Apps.* University of Michigan Press, pp. 188–96.

Reuters. (2022, July 30). Brazil prosecutors ask WhatsApp to delay launch of new tool until January. https://www.reuters.com/world/americas/brazil-prosecutors-ask-whatsapp-delay-launch-new-tool-until-january-2022-07-29/

Reventós, L. (2012, July 9). Inside the world of WhatsApp. *EL PAÍS English Edition*. https://english.elpais.com/elpais/2012/07/09/inenglish/1341836473_977259.htm

Rieder, B. & Sire, G. (2014). Conflicts of interest and incentives to bias: A microeconomic critique of Google's tangled position on the Web. *New Media & Society, 16*(2), 195–211. https://doi.org/10.1177/1461444813481195

Riedl, M.J., Ozawa, J.V.S., Woolley, S. & Garimella, K. (October 2022). Talking politics on WhatsApp: A survey of Cuban, Indian, and Mexican American diaspora communities in the United States. Center for Media Engagement. https://mediaengagement.org/research/whatsapp-politics-cuban-indianmexican-american-communities-in-the-united-states

Rochet, J.-C. & Tirole, J. (2003). Platform competition in two-sided markets. *Journal of the European Economic Association, 1*(4), 990–1029. https://doi.org/10.1162/154247603322493212

Rodriguez, K. & Schoen, S. (August 7, 2020). FAQ: Why Brazil's plan to mandate traceability in private messaging apps will break user's expectation of privacy and security. *Electronic Frontier Foundation*. https://www.eff.org/deeplinks/2020/08/faq-why-brazils-plan-mandate-traceability-private-messaging-apps-will-break-users

Rossini, Stromer-Galley, J., Baptista, E.A. & Veiga de Oliveira, V. (2021). Dysfunctional information sharing on WhatsApp and Facebook: The role of political talk, cross-cutting exposure and social corrections. *New Media & Society, 23*(8), 2430–51. https://doi.org/10.1177/1461444820928059

Rushe, D. (2014). WhatsApp: Facebook acquires messaging service in $19bn deal. *The Guardian*. https://www.theguardian.com/technology/2014/feb/19/facebook-buys-whatsapp-16bn-deal

Saboia, F. (2016, April 15). The rise of WhatsApp in Brazil is about more than just messaging. *Harvard Business Review*. https://hbr.org/2016/04/the-rise-of-whatsapp-in-brazil-is-about-more-than-just-messaging

Santos, M. & Faure, A. (2018). Affordance is power: Contradictions between communicational and technical dimensions of WhatsApp's end-to-end encryption. *Social Media + Society, 4*(3), 2056305118795876. https://doi.org/10.1177/2056305118795876

References

Santos, M., Saldaña, M. & Tsyganova, K. (2021). Subversive affordances as a form of digital transnational activism: The case of Telegram's native proxy. *New Media & Society*, 14614448211054830. https://doi.org/10.1177/14614448211054830

Sarkar, S. (2022). No forwards please. Indian mothers on school WhatsApp groups. In F.J. Green & J.M. Rogers (eds), *Parenting/Internet/Kids: Domesticating Technologies*. Demeter Press, pp. 289–306.

Schwikowski, M. (2021, October 5). WhatsApp and Facebook outage sparks confusion in Africa. https://www.dw.com/en/whatsapp-and-facebook-outage-sparks-confusion-in-africa/a-59411381

Seufert, A., Poignée, F. & Hoßfeld, T. (2022). Pandemic in the digital age: Analyzing WhatsApp communication behavior before, during, and after the COVID-19 lockdown. *Humanities and Social Sciences Communications*, 9, 140. https://doi.org/10.1057/s41599-022-01161-0

Sharples, S. (July 29, 2022). Facebook owner Meta suffers first revenue drop in history, teams will 'shrink'. https://www.news.com.au/finance/business/technology/facebook-owner-meta-suffers-first-revenue-drop-in-history-teams-will-shrink/news-story/ba4e9b98b497f1a8d8cf54a9a7321dbc

Shifman, L. (2014). *Memes in Digital Culture*. MIT Press.

Singh, M. (2020a, March 21). India launches WhatsApp chatbot to create awareness about coronavirus, asks social media services to curb spread of misinformation. *TechCrunch*. https://techcrunch.com/2020/03/21/india-whatsapp-mygov-corona-helpdesk-bot/

Singh, M. (2020b, November 5). WhatsApp rolls out payments in India. *TechCrunch*. https://techcrunch.com/2020/11/05/whatsapp-receives-approval-to-expand-its-payments-service-in-india/

Singh, M. (2020c, June 4). Brazil suspends WhatsApp's payments service. *TechCrunch*. https://techcrunch.com/2020/06/23/brazil-orders-to-suspend-whatsapp-pay-week-after-rollout/

Singh, M. (2022a, October 11). Brands are spamming WhatsApp users in India, Facebook's largest market. *TechCrunch*. https://techcrunch.com/2022/10/10/in-india-businesses-are-increasingly-spamming-users-on-whatsapp/

Singh, M. (2022b, November 18). WhatsApp broadens in-app business directory and search features. *TechCrunch*. https://techcrunch.com/2022/11/17/whatsapp-broadens-in-app-business-directory-and-search-features/

Soares, T. (2023, February 2). How to build a ChatGPT 3 AI Chatbot on WhatsApp. *WhatsApp Business API & Team Inbox*. https://www.wati.io/blog/how-to-build-a-chat-gpt-3-ai-chat-bot-on-whatsapp/

Soeyuenmez, A. (2022, June 30). Indians can now verify their IDs on WhatsApp: Is WhatsApp becoming the 'WeChat of India'? https://www.messengerpeople.com/india-starts-whatsapp-id-verification/

Solon, O. (2017). 'It's digital colonialism': How Facebook's free internet service has failed its users. *The Guardian*. https://www.theguardian.com/technology/2017/jul/27/facebook-free-basics-developing-markets

Sonwalkar, P. (2014, April 4). Lancet study: Prolonged messaging on your smartphone can cause 'WhatsAppitis'. *Hindustan Times*. https://www.hindustantimes.com/health-and-fitness/lancet-study-prolonged-messaging-on-your-smartphone-can-cause-whatsappitis/story-8z0AqGH2vGuehiuxBPSOEL.html

Srnicek, N. (2017). *Platform Capitalism*. Polity.

Staples, L. (2022, November 4). Unfollow? Block? And who gets custody of the WhatsApp groups? How to break up in the digital age. *The Guardian*. https://www.theguardian.com/lifeandstyle/2022/nov/04/how-to-break-up-in-the-digital-age-whatsapp

Statista. (2023, January 23). *Mobile internet usage worldwide – Statistics & Facts*. https://www.statista.com/topics/779/mobile-internet/#topicOverview

Steinberg M. (2020) LINE as Super App: Platformization in East Asia. *Social Media + Society*, 6(2). https://doi.org/10.1177/2056305120933285

Steinberg, M., Mukherjee, R. & Punathembekar, A. (2022). Media power in digital Asia: Super apps and megacorps. *Media, Culture & Society*, 44(8), 1405–19. https://doi.org/10.1177/01634437221127805

Sun, W. & Yu, H. (2020). Wechatting the Australian election: Mandarin-speaking migrants and the teaching of new citizenship practices. *Social Media + Society*, 6(1). https://doi.org/10.1177/2056305120903441

Swart, J., Peters, C. & Broersma, M. (2019). Sharing and discussing news in private social media groups: The social function of news and current affairs in location-based, work-oriented and leisure-focused communities. *Digital Journalism*, 7(2), 187–205. https://doi.org/10.1080/21670811.2018.1465351

Sykes, P. (2018, July 8). The rise of the voice note. *The Sunday Times*. https://www.thetimes.co.uk/article/the-rise-of-the-voice-note-by-pandora-sykes-25shns8rd

Tactical Tech (2018, 3 July). WhatsApp: The widespread use of WhatsApp in political campaigning in the Global South. https://ourdataourselves.tacticaltech.org/posts/whatsapp/

Talmazan, Y. (2021, October 6). Facebook, WhatsApp outage an annoyance for U.S., but a big deal in rest of the world. *NBCNews online*. https://www.nbcnews.com/news/world/facebook-whatsapp-outage-annoyance-u-s-big-deal-rest-world-n1280785

Tandoc, E.C., Lim, D. & Ling, R. (2020). Diffusion of disinformation: How social media users respond to fake news and why. *Journalism*, 21(3), 381–98. https://doi.org/10.1177/1464884919868325

Tapsell, R (2018). The smartphone as the 'weapon of the weak': Assessing the role of communication technologies in Malaysia's regime change. *Journal of Current Southeast Asian Affairs*, 37(3), 9–29. https://doi.org/10.1177/186810341803700302

Tiidenberg, K., Hendry, N.A. & Abidin, C. (2021). *Tumblr*. Polity.

Titcomb, J. (2016, January 24). WhatsApp has a plan to be more than just a messaging app: Will it work? *The Telegraph*. https://www.telegraph.co.uk/technology/news/12116239/WhatsApp-has-a-plan-to-be-more-than-just-a-messaging-app-Will-it-work.html

TNN. (2014, August 1). WhatsApp forward triggers violence in Jaripatka. *The Times of India*. https://timesofindia.indiatimes.com/city/nagpur/whatsapp-forward-triggers-violence-in-jaripatka/articleshow/39381676.cms

Treré, E. (2015). Reclaiming, proclaiming, and maintaining collective identity in the #YoSoy132 movement in Mexico: An examination of digital frontstage and backstage activism through social media and instant messaging platforms. *Information, Communication & Society*, 18(8), 901–15. https://doi.org/10.1080/1369118X.2015.1043744

Treré, E. (2020). The banality of WhatsApp: On the everyday politics of backstage activism in Mexico and Spain. *First Monday*. https://doi.org/10.5210/fm.v25i12.10404

Tynan, D. (2016, August 26). WhatsApp privacy backlash: Facebook angers users by harvesting their data. *The Guardian*. https://www.theguardian.com/technology/2016/aug/25/whatsapp-backlash-facebook-data-privacy-users

Udo, N.S. (2018). The WhatsApp profile photo: Identity representation and visual rhetoric in the digital age. *WritingThreeSixty*, 4(1): 94–112. https://doi.org/10.14426/writing360.v1.329

Vaidhyanathan, S. (2018). *Antisocial Media: How Facebook Disconnects Us and Undermines Democracy*. Oxford University Press.

Valenzuela, S., Bachmann, I. & Bargsted, M. (2021). The personal is the political? What do WhatsApp users share and how it matters for news knowledge, polarization and participation in Chile. *Digital Journalism*, 9(2), 155–75. https://doi.org/10.1080/21670811.2019.1693904

Valeriani, A. & Vaccari, C. (2018). Political talk on mobile instant messaging services: A comparative analysis of Germany, Italy, and the UK. *Information, Communication & Society, 21*(11), 1715–31. https://doi.org/10.1080/1369118X.2017.1350730

van Dijck, J. & Poell, T. (2013) Understanding social media logic. *Media and Communication, 1*(1), 2–14. https://doi.org/10.17645/mac.v1i1.70

Varanasi, R.A., Pal, J. & Vashistha, A. (2022). Accost, accede, or amplify: Attitudes towards COVID-19 misinformation on WhatsApp in India. *CHI Conference on Human Factors in Computing Systems*, 1–17. https://doi.org/10.1145/3491102.3517588

Velasquez, A., Quenette, A.M. & Rojas, H. (2021). WhatsApp political expression and political participation: The role of ethnic minorities' group solidarity and political talk ethnic heterogeneity. *International Journal of Communication, 15*, 2743–64. https://ijoc.org/index.php/ijoc/article/view/15300

Venkataramakrishnan, R. (2015, November 5). This theory explains why Indian Twitter isn't what it used to be – but WhatsApp groups are. *Scroll.In*. http://scroll.in/article/766773/this-theory-explains-why-indian-twitter-isnt-what-it-used-to-be-but-whatsapp-groups-are

Vermeer, S.A.M., Kruikemeier, S., Trilling, D. & de Vreese, C.H. (2021). WhatsApp with politics?! Examining the effects of interpersonal political discussion in instant messaging apps. *The International Journal of Press/Politics, 26*(2), 410–37. https://doi.org/10.1177/1940161220925020

Vincent, J. (2014, November 10). Half of adulterous divorce cases in Italy cite WhatsApp. *The Independent*.

Waldron, T. (2021, October 6). Facebook's 'digital colonialism' made Monday's outage a crisis for the world. *HuffPost*. https://www.huffpost.com/entry/whatsapp-facebook-outage-brazil-africa_n_615c7bc0e4b0548301014544?4m

Wardle, C. & Derakhshan, H. (2017). Information disorder: Toward an interdisciplinary framework for research and policy making. *Council of Europe Report*. https://rm.coe.int/information-disorder-toward-an-interdisciplinary-framework-for-researc/168076277c

Warzel, C. & Mac, R. (2018, December 6). These confidential charts show why Facebook bought WhatsApp. *BuzzFeed*. https://www.buzzfeednews.com/article/charliewarzel/why-facebook-bought-whatsapp

We Are Social. (2022). *Digital 2022 Global Overview Report*. https://wearesocial.com/au/blog/2022/01/digital-2022-another-year-of-bumper-growt

Wei, R. (2008). Motivations for using the mobile phone for mass communications and entertainment. *Telematics and Informatics*, 25(1), 36–46. https://doi.org/10.1016/j.tele.2006.03.001

WhatsApp (2019). Stopping abuse: How WhatsApp fights bulk messaging and automated behavior. https://web.archive.org/web/20190618205325/https://www.whatsapp.com/safety/WA_StoppingAbuse_Whitepaper_020418_Update.pdf

Wilding, R., Baldassar, L., Gamage, S., Worrell, S. & Mohamud, S. (2020) Digital media and the affective economies of transnational families. *International Journal of Cultural Studies*, 23(5), 639–55. https://doi.org/10.1177/1367877920920278

Wodinsky, S. (2021). How WhatsApp swallowed half the world. *Gizmodo*. https://gizmodo.com/how-whatsapp-swallowed-half-the-world-1847805134

Woolley, S.C. & Howard, P.N. (eds) (2019) *Computational Propaganda: Political Parties, Politicians, and Political Manipulation on Social Media*. Oxford University Press.

Yarow, J. (2014, February 20). Here's the inspirational note that the WhatsApp CEO keeps tacked to his desk. *Business Insider*. https://www.businessinsider.com/whatsapp-note-2014-2

Zhong, R. & Satariano, A. (October 8, 2021). Facebook's apps went down. The world saw how much it runs on them. *New York Times*. https://www.nytimes.com/2021/10/05/technology/facebook-down-ig-down-whatsapp-down.html

Zuckerberg, M. (2015, December 28). Free basics protects net neutrality. *Times of India*. https://timesofindia.indiatimes.com/blogs/toi-edit-page/free-basics-protects-net-neutrality/

Zuckerberg, M. (2019a). From town square to living room: Zuckerberg announces sweeping changes to Facebook in new focus on privacy. https://financialpost.com/technology/personal-tech/mark-zuckerberg-announces-sweeping-changes-to-facebook-in-new-focus-on-privacy-encryption

Zuckerberg, M. (2019b). A privacy-focused vision for social networking. Zuckerberg Transcripts, 1006. https://epublications.marquette.edu/zuckerberg_files_transcripts/1006

Index

Page numbers in *italics* refer to figures.

accountability 169
activism 36–7, 104–5, 108–13, 114
Acton, B. and Koum, J. 19, 24–6, 32, 34, 39, 49, 54–5, 57–8, 138–9, 160
admin role in groups 51–2, 81, 84, 114, 122
advertising
   ad-free promise 39, 40–1, 42, 139, 160
   Meta business model 142–3, *144*, 150, 151–2, 160
African countries 3–4, 35, 37–8
   Kenya 67
   Nigeria 115, 123
AI
   algorithmic group segmentation 125
   Business API data gathering 141
   chatbots 149, 163
   group bans 130
   machine learning 65, 66, 121–2
Air France 141
Al Zidjaly, N. 95
Android phones 55, 69
Apple *see* iOS store; iPhone
applification of global culture 22–4
Athique, A. 6, 152
   and Kumar, A. 154
audio messaging 26, 126–7

Australian government
   COVID-19 updates 117–18
   Telecommunications Bill/'encryption bill' 167
automated bulk messaging 124–5

Banaji, S. et al. 50, 54, 120–1, 122
Barcelona, Spain 80, 82, 83–4
   audio messaging 92
   business-oriented features 67
   forwarding messages 63
   group size 50–2
   privacy and encryption 56–7
   research study 4–5
Baulch, E. et al. 20, 76, 122, 123, 126
Baxter, J. 87–9
Bolsonaro, J. 38, 64–5, 122, 125, 126–7
Brazil
   activism 110
   Business Search 72
   and Free Basics 34, 35, 38
   group bans 130
   mobile numbers registered under fraudulent IDs 124
   Presidential election campaign (2018) 38, 64–5, 122, 125, 126–7
   public groups 50, 115
   small business advertising 143

Index

spam 148
'traceability' law 129, 166
WhatsApp Pay: central bank intervention 147
see also Global South
broadcasting/Broadcast lists 66, 104–5, 115–18
shareability and 60–6
Broeker, F. 89–90
Bucher, T. 12, 34, 36, 37, 46, 47, 75, 156, 158
bulk messaging, automated 124–5
Burgess, J.
  and Baym, N. 8, 47, 62, 76, 137, 156, 157
  et al. 12, 166
Business API 70–3, 134, 140–1, 142–3
Business App 69–70, 71–3, 142–3
Business Tools 144
business model and services 66–73, 134–55, 169–71
see also advertising; monetization
business platform 150–3
Business Search 72

Casaes, D. and Córdova, Y. 35, 38, 50, 124, 125
Cathcart, W. 128–9
Chagas, V. 65, 122
chatbots 149, 163
Cheeseman, N. 115
  et al. 123
Chen, Y. et al. 9, 10, 28–9, 30, 77
China *see* WeChat
Christopher, N. 145–6, 148, 149
chunking 87–9
'click to messaging'/'click-to-WhatsApp' ads 142–3, 148
Comey, J. 167
communal/mob violence, India 64, 120–1

Communities feature 53–4, 66
competition *see* superapps
connectedness and disconnectedness 78–9
content moderation 66, 129–30, 166–7
  and encryption 120
  machine learning 65, 66
  core principles 25–6, 39
  ad-free promise 39, 40–1, 42
  COVID-19 pandemic 18, 90
  'CoronaJihad' memes, India 121
  government updates, Australia 117–18
  limiting content sharing 129–30
  stickers 94, 95
  tech sector redundancies 161
  and Zika virus 38

'dark patterns' 149, 150
data
  business-oriented features 68, 141, 149–50, 152
  encryption 49, 54–5
  plans *see* Free Basics
  sharing between WhatsApp and Meta 41–2, 59–60, 142, 172–3
  un-encrypted 55, 58–9, 65
dating apps and texting 89–90
digital colonialism 37–8
  Free Basics and 33–8
digital divide, closing 34, 37
digital wallets and UPI 145–6
document sharing feature 53
Durov, P. 31, 58

East Asian superapps *see* superapps
economic dimension 5–6, 157, 159–60
Electronic Frontier Foundation 168
emojis 94–5

Index

encryption 54–60, 158–9, 165–6
and political activism 111–12
and political manipulation 125
privacy and 13, 31–2, 42, 48–9, 165–6, 170
and regulation 128–9, 166–8
see also privacy
European Union (EU)/ Commission (EC) 42, 57, 128, 129, 172–3
General Data Protection Regulation (GDPR) 149–50
Evangelista, R. and Bruno, F. 122, 124, 125
everyday uses 75–8
and business solutions 147–50
connectedness and disconnectedness 78–9
expressive content 86–99
public display 99–101
see also groups
evolution 156–60
origins and 24–7
exiting groups 96–7
expressive content 86–99

Facebook 12, 33–4, 35, 37–8, 57, 58, 140, 156
#deleteFacebook 42
advertising 142–3, 144
Messenger 4, 26, 30–1, 35, 41, 134–5, 140, 142–3, 157
fact-checking organizations, Africa 38
family groups 80–1
Fishman, A. 24–5
Forward feature 62–5, 115, 119–20
chain mail message 105, *106*
limits 64–5, 66, 120
Free Basics 158
and digital colonialism 33–8
free speech, restrictions on 114

'frontstage' and 'backstage' metaphor 109, 110
future perspective
less simple, reliable and private 163–8
'next chapter' 161–3
as platform 171–3
spammier but still sticky 169–71

General Data Protection Regulation (GDPR), EU 149–50
Gibbs, M. et al. 10, 77, 102
Gillespie, N. 165
Gillespie, T. 8, 49, 62, 71, 76, 106–7, 166–7
et al. 49, 62, 107, 167
global culture, applification of 22–4
Global North 20
Global South 8–9, 19–20, 23, 26
business features and uses 67, 69, 134, 146–7
Free Basics 33–8
groups 50, 54
WhatsApp Pay 144–7
see also specific countries
Global Voices 36, 37
Goggin, G. 22, 23, 29–30, 75, 146, 161, 162
Gómez Cruz, E. and Harindranath, R. 8, 20, 26, 34–5, 170–1
governments
broadcasting 117–18
regulation 128–9, 166–8, 172–3
support of Asian super-apps 29, 152–3
Group feature 48, 49–54
sharing media 62, 66
un-encrypted 55
groups
archetypical behaviours 82–3
family 80–1

mapping exercise 79
strategies for managing 83–6
see also publics and politics
Gursky, J.
et al. 118, 120, 122–3, 125
and Wooley, S. 168

harmful content see
    information disorder
    (misinformation/harmful
    content)
human rights organizations,
    criticisms of Free Basics
    36–8
humour/jokes see stickers and
    memes

India
    business uses and issues 141,
        145–6, 148–9, 169
    Free Basics protests and ban
        36–8
    political uses and issues 64,
        122–3, 125
        COVID-19 pandemic 121
        'traceability' laws 128–9,
            166
        'share' button testing, Twitter
            62
    see also Global South
information disorder
    (misinformation/harmful
    content) 118–19, 167–8
audio messaging 126–7
automated bulk messaging
    124–5
Communities feature 53–4
easy sharing, fast spreading
    and encryption 119–21
forwarding and broadcasting
    63–6, 105
Free Basics 38
management in groups 83–6
networks of trust and political
    manipulation 121–4
see also spam

'instances' 29
use of term 3–4, 11, 12
instant messaging see texting
iOS store 22–3, 24, 25, 30
iPhone 22, 25, 27, 138–9
Ireland: Meta fine 60
Islamophobic memes, India 121
Israel: broadcasting 116

Jio Platforms, India 146
job cuts/redundancies 134, 161
Johns, A. 104–5, 111–12
John, N. 61
jokes/humour see stickers and
    memes
journalism and news
    organizations 113–15

KakaoTalk (South Korea) 27–8,
    29, 32
Kischinhevsky, M. et al. 126–7
Koum, J. 40, 41–2
see also Acton, B. and Koum, J.

'last seen'/'read receipts'
    functions, disabling
    85–6
Latin America
    and Spain 96–9
    see also Brazil; Global South;
        Mexico
LINE (South Korea) 28, 29, 32,
    94
Livingstone, T. 39–40
local 'megacorps' and 'tie-ups'
    146–7

machine learning 65, 66, 121–2
Malaysia (Kuala Lumpur) 79, 81,
    82–3, 84–5, 86
    activism 104–5, 111–12
    everyday uses 92, 93, 95, 96,
        100
    research study 4–5
Maros, A. et al. 127
Matamoros-Fernández, A. 97–9

Matassi, M. et al. 76, 87
media censorship 114
memes and stickers 93–9
Meta
 declining revenues and response 161–2
 job cuts 134, 161
 purchase and development of WhatsApp 33
 stickers 94
 see also future perspective; platform and platformization; *entries beginning* business
Mexico 26, 34–5, 92, 126, 130, 143
#YoSoy132 movement 109
migrant and diasporic communities 90–1
migration to other apps/platforms 170–1
Milan, S. and Barbosa, S. 110, 112, 119
misinformation *see* information disorder (misinformation/harmful content)
mob/communal violence, India 64, 120–1
'mobile first' markets 19–20, 27, 33, 158, 160, 162, 171–2
monetization
 problem 39–43
 quest 138–47, 159–60, 161–2, 172
 see also entries beginning business
Morris, J.W. and Murray, S. 23, 24
multilingual communication 93
'muting' 85–6

Naver (South Korea) 28
'net neutrality' 37
network effects 9, 102, 146–7, 151, 165–6

networks of trust and political manipulation 121–4
New York Times 116
news organizations and journalism 113–15
Nieborg, D.B. and Helmond, A. 3–4, 12, 29, 30, 31, 41, 135, 140, 156, 157
Nigeria 115, 123
Nothias, T. 34, 35, 36, 37

older users 81, 87
Olson, P. 24–5, 41–2
Oman, COVID-19 pandemic 95
Open Whisper 55, 111

paid messaging 139–41
Pay function 144–7
phone contact list 24–5, 123–4
photo- and video-sharing 25
Pierce, D. 91
'platform capitalism' 151
platform and platformization 3–4, 157–60
 analytical framework 5–11
 biography 46–73
 future perspective 171–3
 importance of studying 11–13
 Silicon Valley model 29, 162
 see also entries beginning business
'platform vernacular' 10, 77
plug-in, 'share' button 61–2
politics *see* information disorder (misinformation/harmful content); publics and politics
privacy
 and business features 71–2, 147–50
 see also data; encryption; regulation
private forums and public forums 105–6
profile picture 101
public display 99–101

publics and politics 104–8
  activism 36–7, 104–5, 108–13, 114
  audio messaging 126–7
  automated bulk messaging 124–5
  broadcasting 115–18
  networks of trust and political manipulation 121–4
  news organizations and journalism 113–15
  regulation 127–30
  summary and conclusion 130–3
  see also information disorder (misinformation/harmful content)
push notifications 25, 141
turning off 85–6

racism 97–9
regulation/regulators 127–30
  business platform 137–8, 146, 147
  criticisms of Free Basics 36–8
  governments 128–9, 166–8, 172–3
  National Payments Corporation of India 146
  see also European Union (EU)/Commission (EC)
Reid, A. 116
Rettberg, J.W. 31
Rossini, P. et al. 84, 120
Russia see Telegram

Sandberg, S. 143
Santos, M. and Faure, A. 25–6, 49, 54, 112, 159
Save the Internet (STI) group 36–7
Schneider, T. 116
shareability and broadcast features 60–6
Signal 13, 42, 170

Silicon Valley 'platform' model 29, 162
Snapchat 31
Snowden, E. 110
social dimension 7–11, 157
social media
  definition and WhatsApp fit 12–13
  outage (October 2021) 1–3, 170–1
South Korea see KakaoTalk; LINE
Spain
  15M movement 109
  and Latin America 96–9
  see also Barcelona, Spain
spam 148–50
  stickiness despite 169–71
  see also information disorder (misinformation/harmful content)
Srnicek, N. 150, 151, 152
statuses and profile pictures 99–101
Steinberg, M. 28, 29, 94
  et al. 29, 138, 146–7, 151, 162
stickers and memes 93–9
stickiness 9–11, 43, 77, 169–71
superapps 27–32, 136–7, 145, 152–3, 162
  stickiness 10–11
switching costs 9, 20, 170

technical dimension 6–7, 157, 158–9
Telegram (Russia) 31–2, 58, 112, 170
Terms of Service/Terms and Conditions
  business complaints 169
  updates 72–3
  violations 124–5, 129–30
  terrorism investigations 167
texting 86–90
Titcomb, J. 40
'traceability' laws 129, 166
Treré, E. 109

Twitter 47
  appropriation to incorporation 137
  Koum, #deleteFacebook 42
  responses to social media outage (October 2021) 1–2, 3
  WhatsApp 'share' button testing, India 62

UK
  broadcasting 116
  Online Safety Bill 167
Unified Payments Interface (UPI) 145–6
US 20, 170
  anti-trust cases 172–3
  broadcasting 116
  encryption and regulation 167–8
  Silicon Valley 'platform' model 29, 162

utterance chunking 87–9

video calls 90–1
video-sharing 25
'view once' messages 59
voice calls 87, 90–1
voice/audio messaging 26, 126–7

Wardle, C. and Derakhshan, H. 118, 166
WeChat (China) 28–9, 30, 32, 40
  as 'national champion' 138
  stickiness 9, 10
Wehner, D. 41, 140
Wodinsky, S. 34

Yardley, J. 116

Zuckerberg, M. 13, 34, 35–6, 37, 39, 41, 42, 58, 134–5, 141, 161, 162, 165–6